BREAKING THE MACHO CODE

An Exploration of the Patriarchal Mind and Culture

Paul Hennig

Note for Librarians: A cataloguing record for this book is available from Library and Archives Canada at www.collectionscanada.ca/amicus/index-e.html
ISBN 1-4251-0848-2

Printed on paper with minimum 30% recycled fibre. Trafford's
print shop runs on "green energy" from solar, wind and other environmentally-friendly power
sources.

TRAFFORD
PUBLISHING™

Offices in Canada, USA, Ireland and UK

Book sales for North America and international:
Trafford Publishing, 6E–2333 Government St.,
Victoria, BC V8T 4P4 CANADA
phone 250 383 6864 (toll-free 1 888 232 4444)
fax 250 383 6804; email to orders@trafford.com
Book sales in Europe:
Trafford Publishing (UK) Limited, 9 Park End Street, 2nd Floor
Oxford, UK OX1 1HH UNITED KINGDOM
phone 44 (0)1865 722 113 (local rate 0845 230 9601)
facsimile 44 (0)1865 722 868; info.uk@trafford.com
Order online at:
trafford.com/06-2606

10 9 8 7 6 5 4 3 2 1

CONTENTS

PREFACE

Call the world if you please
                    "The vale of Soul - making."
Then you will find the true use of the world...

                    John Keats

The definition of man
                    is the definition of his soul.

                    Aristotle

Women do not really know as much about men as they think they do. They have developed, over the centuries, considerable expertise in the technique of adapting to men, but that is not the same as truly understanding them. Women often labor under the delusion that life is really pretty easy for men, at least when compared to their own lot, and they have no idea what a complicated struggle is really involved the transition from male childhood to real manhood.

                    Ruth Tiffany Barnhouse, M.D., Th.M.,
                    Harvard University, in her review of He:
                    Understanding Masculine Psychology.

Women think men have it easy because they have power, but there is a curse on that power, like the curse on King Midas, who found that he could not eat food of gold nor recline on a bed of solid gold. In taking power, men have lost touch with the very things they hope to have in their lives: warmth, relationship, love and passionate life. Power, wealth and domination are seductive and corrupting. They obscure a man's vision and judgment and kill his capacity for the very things he seeks. The image on the dust cover of this book is Rouault's "The Old King." This is the face of a man who has given himself over to patriarchal mind and power. It is not a happy face, not the face of a man who has found himself, his bliss, or the answer to the questions and mystery of life.

Sigmund Freud asked, "Women- what do they want?", like they were some kind of tangled, obscure mystery. He might better have asked, "Men- what do they want?" The macho world is a huge fraternity house with a collective lore and culture, notions about manhood, love, sex, relationship and identity. This lore is passed on from generation to generation, but how real is it? How well does it prepare men for the turbulent waters of love, sex, relationship, parenthood and life?

FOREWORD

We men are wounded. The male culture and its macho code of masculinity and selfhood has failed us. It has given us a false and empty model of male identity and selfhood and so we do not know how to accomplish these things. It has failed to prepare us for the turbulent waters of love, life and sexual relationship. These false notions of masculinity and relationship leave us empty, wounded and impotent. Thus wounded, we blindly grope our way through life, failing to fulfill our deep needs for identity, love and relationship. In our pain and emptiness, we lash out at our wives, sons, daughters and other men wounding them in turn.

The collective cultural consciousness has ignored the male wound and its grim consequences for a long time, but ignoring the problem never creates a solution, it is only a desperate hope that it will somehow go away. The macho culture and its code fails to recognize Jung and his essential insights into the psyche, of how we all, men and women, have a masculine and feminine side to ourselves and how essential they both are to our fulfillment. We cannot be complete without both and the psyche is driven to be complete and whole. The macho code teaches us rejection and even contempt for the feminine. It tells us that the feminine is for wimps and faggots. It is not the right stuff.

This neglect of the feminine left me and many men wounded, wounded in our sex. We come to women desperate for her, but in this desperation, we are incapable of balanced, harmonious, deep relationships. We experience our relationships through the context of the need, urgency, pain and unreality generated by the wound. The empty patriarchal code often results in obsession and violence toward women.

This book is my story, my gonzo account of living in the macho world and then trying to understand it, to free myself from it and go beyond it. It is an exploration both within myself and of the culture around us. It is my discovery of the essential insights of Jung, Robert Johnson, Susan Faluti, Teilard de Chardin and a number of other fine writers and thinkers, essential to our understanding of our fulfillment and ourselves. My brother, Ken, who taught me how to write, says, "The only thing we are an authority of is our own experience." So this is my experience of the macho code, the male wound and their effects on my life. How it drove me to pursue a goddess who lived deep down in my psyche. A goddess generated by a phenomena described by Jung as the Anima Projection.

The quest for her destroyed my relationship with a number of fine women. Women who wanted to give me the love and intimacy I desperately wanted and needed, but none of them was the goddess and so I walked away from them. The other variation on the goddess quest plunged me into despair so deep that my life seemed hardly worth living. After one particularly grim relationship, if I had not the psychological and spiritual support I had, I could have killed myself or her and her new lover or all of us. I could have ended up in the newspapers, another sad, strange case with his life ruined.

I have been in the fraternity house, the barracks, the locker room and the bachelor officer's quarters. I have observed and studied our macho male culture and world. I have seen how it fails to prepare us for what Joseph Campbell said about life, "We seek not the meaning of life, but the experience of being fully alive." The macho code fails to show us how to be fully alive. It has been a long journey into this world and its culture. A journey into dark depths, which, at times, seemed bottomless.

When I was at the University of Toronto, Marshal McLuhan said to me, "Most books are like ideas put in a box and all tied up. I want my books to be like a flashlight in a dark room." I hope to have written that kind of book. The macho male world is a dark house with many shadowy rooms. This book is my exploration of this house and its many rooms. Some of the rooms are my personal experience, others are research and sources, which have helped me to understand the depth and impact of the macho mind, and how it shapes us psychologically, politically and socially.

I have looked at my wound and see how it doomed my relationships and distorted my life. I look at how I have begun to heal. Psychology, in its truest sense is a "Knowing of the soul." With this book, I hope to contribute to a knowing of the soul, the knowing of the male soul.

CHAPTER ONE

Cindy and the Goddess

I begin with the stories of three of my relationships. Each one shows a variation on the goddess trip and how I failed to find love and companionship. The story of Cindy and I shows how the goddess undermined the love I could have had with that extraordinary and beautiful woman. I walked away. With Eileen, I was so devastated I scarcely had the will to continue living. With Christina, I was not only devastated, but also murderously enraged. They are all variations of the goddess quest. The opera, "Tales of Hoffman," is the story of his three loves. This is "Tales of Hennig,". I begin with Cindy. The tales are not in chronological order

It was summer of 1966. I was a counsellor at Cradle Beach Camp. Cradle Beach was a wonderful place, on the shore of Lake Erie, south of Buffalo, New York, a summer camp for handicapped kids, disabled kids, disadvantaged kids; in short, any kid with a big problem had a place at Cradle Beach. The counsellors were recruited by "Hops" Allen, the director, from campuses all over the Northeast, but the reputation of the camp traveled and we had counsellors from all over. Hops was a story and a legend all her own.

The counsellors were often social work students, but not necessarily. All were big hearted, big souled young people totally committed to the work and spirit of CBC. They were wonderful, beautiful people and the girls were fabulous.

Cradle Beach was another world, a world the way our world should be, a place of love, compassion, humanity, and a lot of fun. Like the wheelchair football games, where the boys were strapped and padded into their chairs, given helmets and pushed by counsellors who would throw and catch the passes then give the ball to the camper and go with it. It was all crazy and wonderful. The nurse was pretty worried, but it gave those boys an experience they were never going to have. They loved it. It was worth it. There was never an injury.

The games were not brief events. There would be several days of training camp with coaches and secret plays. The girls were given pom-poms and they would learn cheers. The guys were given nicknames like "Big Al" or "Crazy Legs Murphy." Playful creative programs like this were big at CBC and essential for a camp like this where physical activity was limited. After lunch and dinner at the "Big House" there would be, along with the announcements, a brief dramatic presentation like coaches trading insults or a sports commentator, maybe a bookie in from Las Vegas giving odds on the game. All wonderful, crazy stuff. It was another world.

"The Big House" was a long rambling wood frame structure, bluey grey with dark blue trim, basically one floor but with a few staff and storage rooms upstairs. It was perched up on top of a long, high sand dune maybe fifty yards up from the Lake Erie beach. All the main rooms, like the dining hall, kitchen and the rec room had wide screen doors opening out to the long wooden porch running the whole length of the building. The windows on the other side looked down to the beach. No wall was painted an ordinary color. They were the work of past generations of art student counsellors and campers: red and white vertical stripes, mottoes written large on the walls, scenes and cartoons. The decor was totally loose, but perfect. Then Hops' office, the counsellor's lounge and camp office with pictures and posters everywhere. Then a breezeway with a wheelchair ramp down to the beach. Past the breezeway, the laundry room and the nurse's office and the camp bulletin board with the Sunday comics posted every week.

The Big House was the center and heart of camp. For a hundred years, it had shifted and settled down into the sand so that now the floors and walls had a familiar lean, tilt and slope all their own. The Big House, the cabins and the whole of camp even the ground and sand you walked on were saturated with years and years of work, love and dedication. Tragedy, too, because a number of these kids were going to die in a few years, if not the next, but something else was there, too, a kind of celebration of life, even the lives of these kids being lived in the face of very tough odds.

I had heard about Cindy from friends before camp started, then at the pre camp orientation, there she was. Her reputation was well deserved. Cindy was a star at CBC in '64, a great counsellor, respected and loved by the kids and staff. Then she took a year off to work in Kenya with the Peace Corps. Now she was back as supervisor of the Hill, the area of the camp for severely disabled or retarded campers. She was beautiful and vibrant with a dazzling smile, bright eyes, a tall, lean athletic body, and a deep tan complexion. She had that smile for everybody and everybody loved her.

At night, most of the off duty counsellors went to the camp favorite bar, called "down the road." Bars were never my scene so I invited Cindy to walk down to the beach. She talked about Africa. She loved the African culture, the children and their families. Her family didn't like her going to Africa nor did they like Cradle Beach, but Cindy wasn't about to let them stop her from doing what she wanted. Her father was mayor of a small city north of Buffalo. We talked about what a wonderful place Cradle Beach was, our past seasons there and our friends at camp like Bob Goss, one of the great dress up and skit men of all time. A typical Goss getup might be a tie-dye top and black pants tied with an orange sash, black riding boots and a tuba over one shoulder. Goss was a one-man circus and a brilliant artist. This was the Sixties and Cradle Beach was the best of it.

I hadn't been to camp for ten years. I told her about those years, about being a navigator on a RB-66, stationed in Germany and England and then studying for the priest hood in Toronto and teaching at the order's high school in Houston. She talked about her school, Lake Erie College. We had a great walk along the edge of the water and we both felt that we could really talk to each other.

The next night we went down to the beach again. The lifeguard's boat was pulled up on the beach. I told her how John Small, the camp's caretaker had built it in that winter. I showed her the steam bent ribs, the planking and the skill and craft with which John had made it. That boat moved through the water like a dream. My brother, Ken, who was director of the waterfront, spent a lot of time in that boat. He loved it.

I told Cindy about a skit Ken and I had that we would put on when the waves were too high to take the kids swimming. I would walk into the dining hall after lunch with a pair of oars over my shoulder, a turned down sailor hat and a pipe upside down in my mouth and announce,

"I'm Ian McSorly, champeen dinghy surfer. I see the surf's up here at Cradle Beach and I hear you got some overrated surfer guy here who's been trash talking me."

Ken would jump up and say something like, "If anyone's overrated around here it's you, McSorly. As Cradle Beach

Champion Dinghy Surfer, I'm calling you out." (Cheers from loyal fans)

"Well, that's real big talk, Son. I hear you're a family man. Hope your insurance is all paid up. I don't want to be dealing with any widows and orphans."

"You don't have to worry about my insurance, McSorly, you just show up on the beach at the beginning of swim period and we'll have this out." (More cheers)

Dinghy surfing was real good stuff. We would take one of the camp's little 8-foot snub-nosed dinghies and row out in the surf. You had to time it just right, rowing out between the waves, so you could get out past where they were breaking. Then, swinging the boat around, you waited for a good wave and rode the crest in to the beach, but it took quick action with the oars to keep the dinghy from broaching, slewing sidewise, swamping and tumbling in the surf. It was wild. The whole camp would be sitting on the sea wall watching and cheering. We had a judge giving points for the run and keeping score and a sports announcer giving running commentary with a bullhorn. It was so great.

During swim period, Cindy and I would take a couple of kids in the lake together or boating in one of the prams, or we would wheel a couple of wheelchair kids over to the field for crafts. Then, after the kids were in their cabins and in bed, we would go down the beach. I had borrowed a couple sleeping bags from the camping supplies and we would sit on them with our backs to the sea wall and watch the water and talk. I would point out the stars and constellations I had learned from celestial navigation, we would build a little fire and sit around it, or I would light a candle and read a favourite poem. We got closer and closer, and I was kissing her lovely bright face and then caressing her fine body. Then one night we slept on the beach in separate sleeping bags.

The next night I zipped the two bags together and we spent the night like that. It was beautiful, not sexual but close and loving. She was a sweet, loving gal. That went on as we drew closer and closer, but never sexual. We found a little clump of bushes just up on the sea wall, which gave us a nice seclusion. It was very good being that close to a woman that fine. During the week when I was at the University of Toronto studying English, then I came to camp for the three-day weekend, I would write her letters and poems, then give them to her when I got back to camp. I found a few recently.

Night Sounds

The moon silver water
          lay with the gentlest lapping
Against the beach which quietly disappeared
          curving into the water's mist
Hovering over everywhere
          swaddling the whisper of our love
Together with the sound of the night water.

When she was concerned about the difference in our ages, I wrote,

What has age to do
          with the way your fine bright searching soul

scatters bits of sea sparkle light
                    everywhere.
You give me joy and a spreading warmth of hope
                    and we are so good together.

Another time I wrote,

Be of love a little more careful
                              Than of any other thing
But be not afraid, My Girl,
              Love is fragile. thorned flowers
 Desperately beautiful and cruel
Impaling the heart with yearning.
                    Delicate, vulnerable,
              Our flowers bloom anew at every meeting.
A miracle quite beyond merely human us.
O, My Love, believe
                    the splendour of our caress
Was not created to disappear
                    without a trace.

Eventually, she took me home to meet her parents. Cindy was the jewel of her family, twenty-two years old. I was thirty-four, had recently left a Catholic Seminary and was returning to university to get a Master's in Education and teach. I was not what they had in mind for their daughter. Clearly, in their eyes, I was a man of limited means and prospects. Her father was a patrician WASP and mayor of a small city north of Buffalo. He was running for Congress, which he won. Cindy's grandmother would call me, "Mr. Hennig," emphasizing my advanced years. They didn't like Cradle Beach, they didn't like the Peace Corps, and they didn't like me. Cindy didn't care; she just laughed. She ran the family, and they would just have to put up with me. You can see what a jewel I had in Cindy.

During one change over, the three-day rest period between camp sessions, Cindy came up to Toronto to be with me. We stayed at the Windsor Arms hotel near the University campus. I remember the two of us standing nude in front of the full-length mirror in the room and I said, "O Cindy, look at how beautiful we are."

But, still, it was not sexual. I did not understand it at the time. My sexuality was confused and ambivalent. I was coming to Cindy both as a sexual man attracted to her person and beauty, but unconsciously as an infant wanting to be held, suckled and loved by his mother. I wanted the infantile bliss, which I had lost way back as an infant, which now only the goddess of my imagination could seemingly give me. Infantile bliss is way different from sex. It has nothing to do with the genitals. It is Freud's oral stage. Hence, I was fascinated with breasts, not just ordinary breasts, but goddess breasts. It was wonderful with Cindy, she was an extraordinary young woman, mature beyond her years, wonderful, good spirited, beautiful and loving, but through it all, I kept a certain distance. I was in quest of the goddess and goddesses have the breasts of goddesses, which Cindy had not. I was in search of intimacy with a woman who could give me infantile bliss and perfect breasts and beauty was essential.

One time on Wright's beach, Cindy said to me, "Paul, I wish I had breasts for you." Later she said, "Paul, thank you for being you." She was so fine, but I was not capable of taking in the love she offered. I was obsessed with finding the goddess residing deep in my unconscious and I could not settle for anyone less. I was not up to my poetry.

Only much, much later did I come to understand the quest, how it came to be and the genesis of the goddess. My Venus, my goddess was born out of my unconscious, my unconscious wound. The wound struck when I was only year and a half old. My brother was born and displaced me from my mother's attention and affections, or so it seemed.

She was overwhelmed by the birth of a second child so soon after the first and she had little support from my father. He was one more person she had to take care of. Like most patriarchal men, he left the housekeeping, the meals and the children to his wife. Her solution to her overloaded situation was to tell me to go away and be a big boy. She didn't have enough left to meet my needs too. But I wasn't a big boy and I wasn't ready to be one. Feeling my love for her and my need of her was too painful so I pushed all my love and feeling down into my unconscious, but they continued to live down there disconnected from me. I became a survivor. Disconnected from my feelings and the feminine, my unconscious became a fertile ground for the birth of the goddess, a mystical entity who could heal and balm my pain.

Now, as a mature man, my sexuality merged with this mystical entity, my mother goddess. I was in search of a woman who could be both things to me, an impossible role, of course. I was not aware of any of this at the time. What I felt was being pulled two ways. I felt love for Cindy, but I could not fully give myself to her, not emotionally nor sexually. It was like she wasn't the one. She was a compromise and to choose her was to give up the hope of ever finding The One, The Goddess. If I could find her, then I would be able to love. My quest had rendered me impotent. On an even deeper level I was so afraid of suffering that primal hurt again, the old pain of losing my mother, that I could not let myself really love again, so I would either find fault with the woman or I would choose a woman who was emotionally unavailable. I did plenty of that. I was trapped deep down in my unconscious in a Catch-22.

When CBC closed down that summer, we went camping together. Then she went back to her college. I would go down there to see her on the occasional weekend or she would come home and we would see each other. Some times we would spend the night at her family's summer place, "The Stables." It was the beautiful restored and converted stables of a former estate on the edge of the Niagara gorge overlooking the river below the falls. It was good with Cindy. I liked her very much, but I couldn't commit myself to her.

My therapist, John Went, calls the unconscious, "the department of dirty tricks," and by dirty tricks, he means self-destruction and self-denial. With Cindy, I certainly denied myself the relationship and love I so deeply desired. The last I spoke with her was on the phone. She had graduated and was living in Washington where she was working at the Smithsonian. She invited me down to see her during Easter vacation, but I declined. I drifted away and let our relationship die. The last I heard of her was her picture prominently displayed on the Buffalo News society page announcing her engagement to a lawyer in Florida. I'm sure her family was happy. I hope Cindy was and is. I never heard of her again.

I went from one relationship to another locked into the lose lose scenario of the goddess quest. If she wanted a relationship, my feeling for her faded away like it did with Cindy and I drifted away leaving a fine woman hurt and bleeding. If she did not feel for me, then I dropped into a despair so deep I hardly wanted to go on living. Something was very wrong, but I had no idea what it was.

I knew nothing then about the goddess quest. I did not know what I was doing or what was happening. It was all down in my unconscious. The mythological Venus was born out of the sea, lifted up on a giant seashell. In dreams, the sea and water often represents the unconscious. All of which was true for me. Like Groddeck, a confrere of Freud, said. "I was being lived by my unconscious." They don't call it the unconscious for nothing.

All I knew was I really wanted a woman in my life, but it was not happening. It was Catch-22; I couldn't win and it wasn't good.

CHAPTER TWO

The Genesis of the Goddess

My first goddess was Eileen. I was in the seminary, thirty-three years old and not sure if I was going to continue to prepare for the Catholic priesthood. I had taught at one of the Order's high schools, St. Thomas, in Houston for two years and now I was studying theology in the seminary in Toronto. Several of us had volunteered for a program on life and spirituality for high school kids in the local parishes.

We were teamed up with a member of the laity (that is the term priests use for the ordinary folks). I was teamed up with Eileen. She was Irish and vibrantly beautiful with raven black hair, bright blue eyes, an ivory complexion and a fabulous figure. She looked like a goddess. She talked like a goddess. She moved like a goddess. She had the breasts of a goddess. She was a goddess. My heart was in my mouth. We would meet and plan the program. I would prepare slides of photographs and works of art, films, poems, discussions and so on. I was knocking myself out on the program. I was out to impress Eileen and to win her. At this point, I had doubts about continuing with the seminary and the priesthood. I loved the work, the teaching and my classmates in the seminary, but I had serious issues with the Church hierarchy and their positions on women, sex, birth control and spirituality. I was afraid of giving my life over to making people feel guilty, to preaching an oppressive theology having nothing to do with Jesus, and being under the yoke of an institution which had little understanding of what the Christian life and spirituality was truly about.

When I was teaching at St. Thomas, my friend, John Bradshaw, was having a problem with drinking. He had left the Order and was teaching at the local Jesuit high school. His mother called me one evening, in tears, telling me that John was drinking again and hadn't been at the high school for the last two days. Would I go out and try to find him and talk to him? "Yes," I said. She gave me the names of three of his favorite bars. I went to the house superior and told him about John and what I planned to do. Without a word, he opened his desk drawer and pulled out the rulebook of the Order and read me Rule 105. "A religious will rarely leave the house during the week." (This was Tuesday evening and the answer was no.) I said, "I'm going. We'll talk about it later." I walked in the first bar. I was wearing a black suit with a black tie. Some guy at the bar said, "What's this, F.B.I. or C.I.A.?" John wasn't there. He wasn't at any of the others either. But the next night one of the bartenders told John that there was a guy with red hair and a black suit looking for him. John knew it was me and he sobered up, went back to the high school and salvaged his job.

But I was stunned that my superior could think the way he did, and it rocked my confidence in the institution of the Church. So when Eileen came along she tipped the scales. We would meet to plan the weekly presentations sometimes in the seminary, other times at a coffee house in Yorkville. This was the sixties before the developers ruined Yorkville. There was the Penny Farthing. Joni Mitchell was singing at the Riverboat. It was so great. I was thirty-three and she was nineteen, but a wonderfully mature, intelligent, soulful nineteen. By now, it was December and one night Eileen called me at the seminary and said,

"I have to see you tonight. There is something I have to tell you."

"Sure," I said, "I can be in Queen's Park at eight o'clock."

I waited for her under a tree in the park. It was a clear, starry, winter night. Then she came running across the park through the snow. I came out to meet her as she ran into my arms, gave me a flower, held me, kissed me and said,

"I love you, but don't love me. I'll only hurt you." I was thrilled, totally in love with her. I didn't know what to make of what she said. I kissed her back and said,

"Don't worry. I am a big boy. I can take care of myself." I was so very happy. I know now she was warning me, somewhere she knew, but I knew nothing then.

We would meet every chance we could. In a letter, she called me her tambourine man. "Hey, Mr. Tambourine Man play a song for me. In the jingle jangle morning I'll come following you." O, Lordy, yes! It was wonderful. With her, I felt like every cell of my body was loving her and was vibrating with ecstasy. I had never experienced anything like it. We would attend planning sessions in the seminary for all the members of the program. No one knew of our relationship. I would be in my cassock and Roman collar. During the meetings, we would exchange a secret glance or a touch under the table. We would meet in the afternoons. It was winter and cold. We would go into churches, climb the stairs up to the balcony and hold each other and talk and kiss.

Yorkville in those days had a lovely little art gallery, the Atelier. I took her there to an exhibit of Chagall's "Dauphus and Chloe" paintings. She loved them. It was beautiful. We were like the two lovers in Chagall's paintings. We both felt that ours was a profound love. It was total bliss. I had my goddess in my arms. We were both very Catholic so there could be no "sinful" touches or kisses, but we were on the edge.

She was the goddess with the magic power to melt my frozen feelings and I was alive again. It was like a spring thaw and the rush of feeling was a joy and a fullness the like of which I had never known before, but it was doomed. Then she said something I couldn't understand, "I stay up every night until midnight so I will get in to the next day still loving you." What was that? I asked myself, but I did not ask her.

Then the nightmares began, she told me, "I fall asleep and dream the same dream over and over, I am standing on a dock and a huge snake rears up from the water and drags me off the dock and down under the water." I was heartsick to hear it. I knew we were in trouble. Then she began having doubts about our relationship. She would ask, "Is it real?" I didn't know how to answer that. I know now she was asking, "Is what we feel for each other real? Is our relationship real? Can I trust it?" She became more and more distant and doubtful. I was devastated. I couldn't talk to her. I couldn't bear to be with her feeling so empty. I felt gutted, hollowed out. I didn't know how I was going to live. I would have gone to the ends of the earth for her. I would have given my life for her. She was my goddess and I had lost her.

Now things she had told me began to fall into place. How her charming Irish father would win her love then drink and turn nasty and go off to his parties with his drinking friends and other women. Then he would be sorry, beg her forgiveness and be the charming self. Then do it all over again. He would love her, and then betray her and her mother. Then love them again, win their love, and then betray that love, over and over again. She told me of last Christmas when he gave her a record player which she loved.

She was a very talented folk singer and with the record player, she could sing and play along with her favorite singers like Joan Baez and Joni Mitchell. That New Year's Eve he wanted to take the player to one of his drunken parties. She wouldn't give it to him. There was a struggle and the record player was broken. What a nightmare. No wonder she could not trust the love of a man or her love of him. I was dying inside. She was gone. I found this in my journal years later, "The sun is gone from my winter sky." It was all over and she was gone.

I had heaven on earth and it was a long way down. I had relived my history with my mother. I had her for a time and then lost her. I had the bliss, the joy and the security of her love, then it was taken away. I wanted and needed Eileen as I wanted and needed my mother when I was one and a half years old and I was just as devastated as when I lost her then. Slowly over the months, I put my life back together the best that I could. That was what it was like, putting the pieces back together.

CHAPTER THREE

In the Shadow of the Goddess

Christine was my most serious goddess projection. I could have blown my sanity and ended up in the newspapers with my life ruined over her. It all started at Ariel's birthday party, a playmate of my five-year-old son, Jesse. It was the fall of 1986. Linda and I had Jesse. We tried living together when Jesse was quite young, but we were never in love. We lived together because we loved Jesse, but it didn't work. Linda, with Jesse, moved out after a year and a half. I was sorry to see them go, but it had to be. A year or so later, She met and married Russell, but I saw Jesse several times a week and shared in his parenting. Jesse is the best thing that ever happened to me in my whole life.

Linda had dropped Jesse off at the party earlier, and I was to take him back to my place when the party was over, back to my boat. I was living on Wizard down at Harbour front. I knocked at the door of a townhouse in an older, upscale neighborhood of Toronto. Ariel's father, answered, introduced himself, and let me in. I soon found Jesse, but he was busy with his little friends. After I greeted him, I was admiring the rather good impressionist reproductions on the wall of the room when I noticed a striking woman across the room. Her eyes struck me big, wide and blue with a bright, innocent look like a child's. Her body was full and well formed and she was not wearing a ring. Linda and I had ceased being a couple three years ago, and there hadn't been a woman in my life since. Striking up conversations with beautiful strangers has never been my forte, but I had to try.

Feeling quite obvious, I walked over to her, introduced myself and began chatting about Jesse, the party and parenting. She talked about her son, Paul. She was easy to talk to, warm, pleasantly engaging, intelligent with a lovely smile. When the party was over and it was time to leave, I said, "Christina, I've enjoyed meeting you and talking with you. The trouble with the big city is I'll probably never see you again unless I call you. May I?" She hesitated a moment and said, "I don't have a phone, but I'm at my mother's most afternoons you could call me there." She gave me the number then left with her father, who was at the party with her.

I was excited. I was twice her age, but so what. I called a few days later. We had another easy, warm, interesting conversation. I asked her out and she said to call back in a week. A week later, I called. We talked awhile and then she invited me over to her parent's house the following week. I was curious where she lived and why everything took place at her parent's place, but I felt it would be awkward to ask. The following week I went over there. It was a big old house near High Park. We played with her three kids in the backyard: Krina, 5, Paul, 4, and Michael, 1. I'm at ease with children. I liked them and they liked me. We all had lunch together. It was all really very nice. Christina moves with an easy athletic grace. She was an interesting, vital, beautiful woman.

The next week I was working on my boat, Wizard, a 48' Yawl, on which I ran a big boat sailing school and charter boat business. I had hauled out her out and I was racing with the October weather to replace a couple of hull planks. I was working on the boat when she came walking toward the boat pushing Michael in his stroller. I could hardly believe it. I showed her the boat and the work I was doing. I had taken two planks out exposing the ribs of the boat. Work on a wood boat is always interesting, and I'm proud of what I can do. There aren't many guys left who can do serious work on wood boats.

Then I walked her and Michael back to her car and she asked me why I hadn't called. I was blown away. It had been only a week. I made a lame excuse about having to get the boat finished before the weather turned bad, but the truth was I didn't want to look like I was coming on too strong. I called the next day. Her mother answered the phone and told me Christina was not there and then she invited me to dinner in a couple of days. Naturally, I said "yes."

That evening I found myself at dinner with Christina and her parents. Her mother was quite talkative and carried most of the conversation. I filled in with stories about sailing and Wizard, and my former teaching career. Christina's father was a bit quiet, but pleasant enough, content to let his wife do most of the talking. He was a teacher of mathematics at a local community college, and we had that in common, as I had taught math and physics. Christina was rather quiet, letting the rest of us carry the conversation. After dinner, we were all having a liqueur when her mother invited me to a weekend at their cottage in two weeks' time. I wondered what Christina thought of this and why the invitation was not coming from her, but I wasn't going to ask any questions. I accepted with thanks and anticipation.

As the weekend approached, I was curious what was going to happen. Christina and I hadn't had much of a chance to be alone and really talk. Nearly all our time together had been with the children or with her parents. It had all been very quiet, polite and pleasant. The weekend arrived and that Friday afternoon Christina and I loaded the kids, all their gear and our luggage into her father's car. It all felt very domestic. Both her parents had gone ahead in her mother's car. We drove up in the bright autumn sunshine. On the way up to the cottage, I pointed out the Durham County Forest, one of my favorite cross-country ski trails not far from the cottage. After we arrived at the cottage and unloaded the car, we left the children with her parents and took a walk.

The cottage was in a compound of maybe thirty cottages of Estonian families who all knew each other. Perhaps the birch and evergreen trees reminded them of the land they had come from. Then we came to the summer camp. The stream was dammed up to make a small lake where the kids could swim and canoe. Christina had gone there as a child and a teenager, then as a counsellor. It was all a tidy, pretty little place, probably the realization of a lot of dreams for the parents, but I got the sense that for a restless, creative spirit like Christina, it was too closed and small a world.

That evening we were all at dinner. She was so beautiful with her wide, bright smile. She looked like a small, maybe 5'5", Marilyn Monroe. Her body was very well conditioned. Later I learned that she had been a national class gymnast in her teens, and that conditioning was still with her. I was so cranked I could hardly eat dinner. After dinner, we all watched TV, and then we put the three children to bed. Eventually her mother and father went to bed and we were finally alone. I noticed her rubbing her neck. I asked her about it. She said it was quite stiff. I told her I was a good amateur masseuse and perhaps I could help.

We went into my room, and she lay face down on my bed. I straddled her between my knees and began kneading her neck on either side of the vertebrae, then down between her shoulder blades then all the down her back, then her feet and calves. I could feel her relaxing and enjoying it. Her body was wonderful, and my heart was pounding in my throat. I flexed her legs at the knee and kneaded the backs of her knees, then her thighs. So beautiful and she didn't object. I worked my hands under her shirt and ran them up her bare back and across her shoulders. Then I lay gently on her reaching over to kiss her cheek. I could feel her turning under me. I lifted myself up to let her turn then, as she turned, she kissed me eagerly on the mouth. I was thrilled; all my hopes and longing were coming true. Soon we were doing some serious rolling around and we were nude in the bed together. Then she was on her hands and knees over me, like a beautiful female animal, her full, rounded breasts hanging in cones like the she wolf of Rome nursing her cubs, Remus and Romulus.

Then she said, "I promised my father I wouldn't do this." Well, we didn't have any precautions so not much more could happen. She got up and went to her room. A couple minutes later, she reappeared, standing in the doorway wearing this flannel nighty and smiling her wonderful smile with her eyes kind of squinty. I crossed over to her and kissed her and caressed her under the soft flannel. It was so sexy in this very homey way that I could not stop smiling down into her face looking back at me with her radiant smile. I was so happy and thrilled. It felt like every cell of my body was vibrating with joy. Perhaps I had found the goddess whom I had been searching for all these years. I was wildly happy.

The next day we were driving around exploring the countryside when she began to talk. She was desperately unhappy all through her adolescence: an empty routine of Estonian cultural events and classes, piano lessons, gymnastics and a private, toney girl's school, Bishop Strachan, which she hated. None of it was her. At eighteen, she took a trip to New York City where she met George, who told her he and his friends, "would chew her up for breakfast and spit her out." Nevertheless, she is intrigued by him. A little later, she runs away from home and takes off with him. They are into drugs. They make their way to Florida. They run out of money, and they are eating in soup kitchens. Then they were arrested for breaking and entering.

Somehow, during all this Christina bears him Kirina and a pair of twins, Paul and Annabel. Four months after the twins are born, George was taking care of them alone when Annabel starts vomiting. Four hours later, he takes her to the hospital where she dies of head injuries. He maintains he accidentally dropped her. The hospital is suspicious and so is Christina, but there is no evidence and no charges. Christina runs home to her parents with the children. But she makes up with George and runs off with him again, leaving the children with her parents who take legal custody. Sometime later George and Christina come back for the children. The parents say, no, they do not trust them. They take the children anyhow and run to the states. Her parents charge them with abduction. They are caught and convicted. George is ordered by the court never to see the children and to never enter Canada. Christina is placed on probation and in the care of her parents and ordered to seek therapy.

She ran off again to George, married him and bore him Michael. Finally, she wakes up when she sees George, in an insane rage, chasing his mother around the kitchen with a carving knife. She takes Michael and runs to her parent's home in Canada. George follows her, lurks around the house, and threatens her with phone calls and mail. They call the police. George is taken to the border and deported with a restraining order.

Christina was driving while she told me this like it was a

bad dream that is finally over. Her little face is so wide and trusting. I could see her so clearly at eighteen, naive, having no idea of the pitfalls, no idea of how difficult it is to escape from the craziness. I could see her in the middle of this nightmare not knowing how she got there or how it could have happened. Now with all this having fallen down around her like house of cards, she was rebuilding her life. She seemed brave and hopeful now, and my heart went out to her. I was moved that she trusted me to confide all this. I so wanted to replace this horror with real love, caring and joy that I could hardly swallow. I wanted to help her heal all this and to be with her while she was doing it.

After that weekend, we saw a lot of each other. In the car she would snuggle up to me and I would put my arm around her and drive with one hand while she shifted the gears. I felt like a teenager. When I would pick her up at the house, we would get into the car and she would turn to me with her face up to be kissed and I would kiss her and her face would still be up to mine and she would gently tug at my collar to pull me down to her again. It was wonderful.

Wizard was back in the water now and I had a little party on board for her. I was proud to introduce her to my friends: Carl and Dale, Les, Ian, Carol and Stefanie. Christina gave me this funny little Santa Claus, which I hung from the cabin light. We listened to Stan Rogers and Dire Straits and talked and drank and laughed. It was so great. I took her home and she invited me in and made tea which she took into the living room. She did not turn on the lights but lit a candle instead. All this was done with great care and no trace of hurry like a ceremony. We sat on the couch and talked and sipped our tea and then began to kiss and hold each other. We spent the night together sleeping and making love on the cushions spread out on the living room floor while her parents and children slept upstairs. Every couple of hours I would say, "I should go now," and she would say, "No, stay." I had never felt like this in my life. It was total bliss. The living room windows began to go light and still we lingered. Then we heard the children coming down the stairs. I jumped up, leapt into my clothes and scurried out the front door, just in time.

A week later, it was her mother's birthday. Christina planned a lovely surprise party at her apartment. She invited relatives and friends of her mother's. It was so fine to see Christina doing this. It was as if she was healing old wounds with her mother. I helped her to find a hand-embroidered pillow that her mother liked very much. The party was a great success. Both Christina and her mother loved it. Her mother was moved that Christina had taken such care. I stayed until everyone else had left and helped Christina clean up and then we went to bed, her bed with its beautiful sheets and pillows. It was wonderful.

Every time we were together, we came to know each other more and more and it kept getting better and better. In the morning, I helped her change Michael. I felt married and it felt very good. I could see us and the kids, living together, going camping, playing baseball, and having a rich life together.

A few days later, Christina called me and said she saw George standing in the backyard. She was frightened and asked me to come over. I jumped into my car and raced over. He was gone when I got there, but I stayed with her the afternoon. She had turned to me for protection, and I was very happy to be there for her. She called the police, who later picked him up and detained him.

Then a couple interesting connections occurred. When I told her my middle name was Michael she was quite moved, as Paul and Michael are the names of her two boys. Then she called an old friend, Debbie, a lawyer who had helped her a couple years ago with her legal problems. I knew Debbie from years ago and she gave me a glowing recommendation. In the big city, this was an amazing coincidence. It felt like good omens.

Christina was a terrific artist. One afternoon she showed me some things she had done. First, her work from high school, that swank girl's school. Her art teacher said to her, "We have never had anything like this in the school before." I could well imagine not; it was wild, original work right out of the depths of her. It was like Edvard Monk, maybe even better. She showed me a portrait of her, George and Karina, painted while they were together and supposedly in good space. Christina was half sitting, half cowering at George's feet while she held Karina to her. The background was dark and ominous. Christina and Karina are bright in whites and yellows. George was looming over them, his form dark with a greyish, purple face, menacing and horrible. Christina said, "I couldn't paint him any other color." The eyes, huge, sunken and hollow painted in spinning vortexes of white and yellow, a soundless scream in their mouths. It was like looking into three raw souls, terrible, but it was the real goods.

It was utterly incredible, somewhere she knew, deep inside of her, just what was going on. She was working on a portrait of herself, the children and me. She wanted to live in a studio so she could paint while taking care of the children. I felt that could be very good. She was good enough to make a living at her art. I knew a few artists who lived in their studios, so I took her around to meet them and see their studios. She liked the looks of it. Then we looked at some empty warehouse space, which could be converted into a live in studio. I loved the prospect of helping Christina to do this and then building tables out of cable drums, shelves and cupboards and closets out of packing crate lumber and living there with her and the children. It was exciting.

We were seeing a lot of each other. Every evening when I would bring her home, we would have our little tea ceremony. She would set out the cups, light candles, turn out the lights, and then pour the tea. It was so lovely. One night with the lights off and the room bathed in candlelight a strange thing happened. Her beautiful, wide-eyed, smiling face changed into another face like hers, but now aged and ravaged by years and years of heavy and terrible living, a face hardened, bloated and emptied by bad times and years of all night drinking and smoke filled rooms, her eyes empty and lifeless. Her youth totally gone. What was I seeing? Was I seeing things? Was it the candlelight? I looked hard into her face, No, it was there. I was not imagining this. After a few moments, her lovely, smiling face came back. I was shaken. Where had this apparition come from? What I should have asked was, "What is it telling me?"

Soon the Christmas season was upon us. Her family is close knit and there were a number of family gatherings with dinner and lots of people for hours on end, so there was not much time for us to be together or to really talk. But there in the midst of all the relatives, Christina would gently, secretly brush by me with her hip or breasts or trailing her finger tips down my back. With this, I could endure the relatives for hours. Actually, I liked them. They were good solid people. I didn't mind even when they spoke Estonian, and I could understand nothing. The feeling in the room was good. I think her grandmother liked me. She invited us up to her farm in Huntsville. It felt like something was building between us.

During this time, Linda, her husband, Russell with Jesse, had moved to Thunder Bay, eighteen hundred miles away. Our last night together in Toronto was the hardest time I have ever had. We both knew things would never be the same.

Now he was flying down to be with me for the holidays. I met him at the airport and we went directly to Buffalo to be with my family for Christmas. When we got back we got together with Christina and her children, but having Jesse with me all the time made it hard to have any time alone with Christina. Finally, I arranged for Jesse to have a sleep over with a friend so Christina and I could go out. We got into the car and I was looking forward to our little ritual of her face turned up to be kissed again and again and the little tugs on my collar, but it was not there. She just sat there submitting saying nothing. Stunned, I drove to the movie down at the Beaches and walked along the icy water's edge. I held her and kissed her, but there was nothing from her to warm the chill from the lake. I asked her what was wrong. She answered vaguely about me being too serious and that she was feeling depressed.

I instantly realized that I had made a big mistake in letting things move so rapidly. All that time together, all those family gatherings and dinners, night after night, like we were married. Of course, it was too much, too soon. It was all overwhelming and now she was pulling away. We went to the movie we had planned to see, "The Gods Must Be Crazy," a very nice movie, but the chill between us made it painful for me to sit there. After the show, we drove back to her place in silence. As she was about to get out of the car, I said,

"It looks like it would be better if we didn't see each other for a little while. How about if I call you in a week and we see how things are?"

She said, "All right."

Then I said, "Is it all gone? All the good stuff we have had together?"

"No, I just need some time to get over this stuff."

Five days later, I sent her daisies, and then two days later with my heart in my mouth, I called her. We had a very nice chat. She talked of how it had been only nine months since she had left George and how she needed time to recover. She was warm and lovely and making perfect sense. Again, I could see how I had come on too strong, too fast, like when I was helping her to find a studio; I said I would love to live there with her and the children. I had said, "I would love to have a child with you, Christina." She seemed glad to hear that from me and I was deeply moved. I wanted that with her very much, but it was all too much, too fast. Then she said, "How did you know that daisies are my favorite flower?" "They just seemed to be your kind of flower."

She invited me to Michael's first birthday party the next day, and we talked about maybe going to a movie after the party. I was thrilled and hopeful and went out to buy a present for Michael. I found a great little train locomotive with see through gears and engine. The next day I arrived at the party at about two in the afternoon. Hour after hour went by relatives, the children, the food. Christina was polite and occasionally smiled but always with a hidden distance. I asked her to dance. She got up without saying anything and danced without looking at me, a million miles away. I stopped dancing and said,

"Looks like we're not going to that movie."

"What movie?"

"Yesterday, on the phone we talked about maybe going to a movie if the party ended early."

"No, we didn't."

She spoke with a negative chill in her voice and eyes. All totally unnecessary. All she had to say was, "I don't remember that and anyway the party is going to run too late for that." Instead, she was manufacturing this ugly exchange. I said, "That's not important. What is important is what is going on here and now. I want to talk to you alone." We went downstairs to the laundry room in the basement. I don't remember everything that was said. I remember her eyes and face and voice flat, hard and cutting. She was another person. A person I had never seen before. She said, "I'm fickle and that's that." It was as though all our beautiful times together had never happened. They were gone like smoke in the wind. Our lovely, hopeful talk of only yesterday, all of it gone. I walked out of the house, torn and bleeding.

The next week passed in misery, then I called her. I said, "I regret the way I said some of the things I said. They came out through hurt and anger. She felt much the same way. It was a good talk and I felt a little more hopeful. She said to call her in a week and we could get together for a talk.

A week later, I called. We chatted and arranged to get together Sunday afternoon. She asked me not to come to the house, but to meet her near the park four blocks away. I was puzzled, but I was not going to question her. That Sunday afternoon I went cross-country skiing first. I had to do something else that day other than just see her. It was one of those beautiful sun filled blue-sky, snowy days, perfect for skiing. I felt good or as good as I was going to feel with the anxiety of meeting her, and I looked good with a leather vest over my heavy winter sweater, a blue bandanna around my forehead and thick corduroy trousers.

I drove up to the church on the corner right at three thirty. She was already there wearing sunglasses I had never seen before. She got into the car. I chatted about what a terrific day it was, asked about the kids. The park wasn't far. I parked the car and we walked through a stand of evergreens while I read to her a letter I had written to her. In the letter I said, even if things between us have changed, no matter what form our relationship takes, I would always love her and treasure what we have had together. When I finished reading it there was a moment and then she said, "I'm glad it wasn't longer. I might have cried."

As we silently walked along, every now and then a strange wave of feeling would pass over her face distorting her beautiful face. We came to the park restaurant, went in, ordered tea and toast and began to talk. She told me she had been to a party recently where she met her first boyfriend, the first guy she had gone to bed with, and he hardly talked to her. He had nothing for her. She couldn't understand it. Well, I could. She talked about him about a month ago, how he wouldn't have sex with her unless she took LSD first. Clearly, a lovely boy. Once again, I saw her, a beautiful teenager, wide-eyed, trusting, and naïve; she had no idea. On top of this, she has a penchant for picking bad-news guys. I said, "A beautiful woman like you is prey to guys like that. You are nothing more than meat to them. There is a vast difference between making love and having sex. They are not always the same thing."

I asked her to take off her sunglasses because I couldn't see her eyes. She did. Her eyes were, as I had never seen them, empty and flat. That wondrous light was entirely gone. Then she turned to me and tried to smile, her bright smile, but it failed. A few minutes later, when she thought I wasn't looking that strange wave passed again over her face. I told her about the locker room, the fraternity house, and that ugly, macho, belt-notching scene where a beautiful woman is a trophy and how these guys would crow about screwing her brains out, their term for that profound moment when a woman totally surrenders herself to a man.

I told her about Charlie, a guy I knew in the Air Force when I was stationed in England. Charlie, two of our friends and I rented a big, old manor house. There were stables, rolling lawns, a boathouse on the riverbank. It was like living back in Edwardian England. We were young officers and there were parties, terrific parties. Charlie was the chief organizer. He could really put it together—the music, the drinks, the food, everything. Charlie was very good with the girls, that is to say successful, with lots of them. He was charming, witty, and clever. He was Mr. Goodtimes himself, and the girls loved it. He was a masterful seducer. None of us had ever seen anything like him.

He had this little game he would play. He would be with a pretty girl at one of our parties, chatting, smiling, laughing, and skilfully entertaining her. Then he would turn to us, his buddies, smile, and say, " JAC," which was his code word for "Just another cunt." Christina asked, "Why?"

"A friend of mine defines duplicity as, 'What you see is not what is going on,' and what was going under Charlie's smiles and charm was a total contempt and hostility toward women."

" Again Why?"

"Men, like Charlie, need women to prop themselves up and because they need women, they must manipulate them, put them down, even humiliate them, in order to convince themselves of their power over them. It's a nasty business. I doubt if they themselves understand why they do what they do. It's all unconscious, but that doesn't make it any less nasty."

We talked and talked, two hours flew by and then she

had to go. I paid the bill and we walked outside under the pines. I said,

"Things just moved too fast. We need breathing space," and that I was seeing someone else as well. I told her that a year ago, I had given up hope of ever having a woman in my life and that she had shaken me out of that despair and that now I was not going to settle for a life without love." She said, "I hope someday I'll be more than an inspiration."

This was all feeling pretty good and those waves of strange feeling across her face had stopped some time ago and she had her old beautiful smile again. As I was driving her home, she asked, "What would you think if someone said that everything you say is bullshit?"

"Well, that's a real put down. I'd seriously think about how he feels about women."

She was thoughtful after that. I thought to myself, she is seeing some bastard who said that to her. I pulled the car into her driveway. We both said it had been a terrific afternoon. As she moved to get out of the car, she quickly kissed me on the mouth and went into the house. All that felt good. I was very encouraged. It really had been a terrific afternoon, filled with feelings and vibrant conversation. I couldn't remember when I'd had a conversation like that. Well, if we were capable of stimulating that kind of energy in each other something must be there alive and kicking.

I decided to go for the long haul. I would back off our relationship to a friendship with meetings like this and give her time to run through this affair with this son-of-a-bitch who was telling her that everything she says is bullshit. Hopefully, in time, she would come to see the value of what I had to give her.

A week later, I called her. We chatted and I asked her if she wanted to get together. She said yes that Sunday after she put Michael to bed. I took her to this fine little café in the Kensington Market. It could have been some place on the Left Bank of the Seine. She loved it. We had another terrific conversation, a beautiful, rich, stimulating conversation. At one point she asked,

"How can I have a man in my life with three kids."

I assured her that she could if she chose the right man, hoping as I said it that she would see that I am the kind of man. The she asked if it were possible to have "wild times" in her life? I said, "Yes." But I was thinking to myself, "That depends on what kind of wild times you have in mind." I wondered just what kind of wild times she had in mind, but I didn't have the guts to ask. Then she asked if I had read Nietzsche. "Yes", I said. She smiled as if my affirmation of these things was good. But I was thinking, The last thing you need is a half-baked reading of Nietzsche, but, again, I didn't have the guts to ask her what she understood from Nietzsche, but I was going to re-read Nietzsche and pick out some of his better passages like, " The most important thing in marriage is not sex, but conversation." Yeah, the kind of conversations we have been having. On the way home, she complained about how her mother and sister were all over her about seeing this guy. We got home and she invited me in for tea which she prepared with the old ceremony and lit candles in the living room. It felt good and I felt that what we had together was not all gone.

A couple of weeks later, she called me at my office to tell me she wanted to look for a studio again, and asked me to help her. Great, I thought to myself as I said, "Sure, I'll call a friend of mine who is a commercial real estate agent and see if there is some interesting warehouse space around."

She thanked me warmly. I called my friend. Yes, a well-finished warehouse was available. I drew up a plan where

Christina takes 7,000 sq. ft, divides it up into five studios and sub-lets four of them, and gets hers for a third of the rent. That Thursday, I picked her up after work and we looked at the warehouse. It was good and adaptable to the plan. She was excited by the possibilities of it and thanked me. We made plans to take the kids to Toronto Island that Sunday, but when I suggested picking her and the kids up at her parents' house, she became uncomfortable and that strange wave of feeling came over her face and distorting it. She insisted that we meet at the ferry docks. I was curious what this was all about. I pointed out that she had never been to the docks before, and that there would be a lot of people there. It was a difficult place to meet and we could easily miss each other. But she anxiously insisted, so we had to meet at the docks.

The next day I had a strange premonition that something was wrong and I kept trying to reach her by phone, but there was no answer, which was strange because she was taking care of the kids. Finally, at about 6:00 her mother answered the phone. She was in tears and it all tumbled out. A half-hour ago, Christina and John, this new boyfriend, came home with the children. John was falling down drunk, Christina had been drinking as well, and the kids were wet and cold from all day in the snowy, wet park. She threw John out of the house and Christina went with him. Then she told me what was going on. They rented out three rooms to three men up on their third floor. During the Christmas holidays when I was in Buffalo visiting my family, Christina went up there and met this John. Since then she had been going up there all night with him drinking and God-knows-what-else.

Later I found out that this guy was a major fan of punk rock, a Billy Idol wannabe. So, in the morning, after a big night of drinking, punk rock and whatever else, she would come down to take care of the kids, but she would sleep half the day while the children were just left to themselves. Kirina was closing herself in cupboards and sucking her thumbs all day like she used to. Through her tears her mother said, "He is just like George and she is just like she was then."

"She is just like she was then," I was sick to hear it. The nightmare has returned. She was back to what she was with George. Her dark self had come back...a number of things fell in place: those strange waves of feeling which would pass over her face, distorting it, her anxiety over my coming to the house. She did not want this guy to see me with her. Now I knew what she meant by "wild times." The answer is: not your kind of wild times. The beautiful thing I thought I had with her was a shimmering unreality. It had no substance. It was all nothing to her and nothing for me.

I anguished over all this for hours. Then I had to talk to her. For some strange reason I had to hear from her. I knew they would go to her apartment in Rexdale. I dialled her number planning to pretend I knew nothing of what had happened and that I was merely calling about out upcoming trip to Toronto Island. The phone rang and Mr. Punk Rocker answered,

"Hello."

"May I speak to Christina?"

"Who's this?" He demanded in this harsh sullen voice. Everything he was came through his voice. I was sick at the sound of it.

"Paul", I answered. Silence for a moment, and then Christina came on the line.

"Hi, Christina, how are you? Beautiful day wasn't it."

"No! It was a horrible day. My parents are all over me again. They threw me out of the house. O, God, they are so impossible." She went on a bit, and then there was this strange sound over the phone, like a dog panting. It must have been Mr. Punk Rocker. There was a pause, and then she laughed this horrible ugly laugh. Then I heard the phone dropped and left hanging on the wall. Then over the still live phone at a distance, I heard her laugh again, a drunken whore's laugh. I was out of my skull with rage, hurt, insult and humiliation. Of course, I had set myself up for it. For some reason beyond explanation, I got up, pulled on my parka, grabbed my car keys and climbed off the boat. I got to my car and drove to her apartment in a murderous rage. I could have gladly slaughtered the both of them.

I arrived at the house where she had a basement apartment, parking my car a few doors away. I carefully checked the street for anyone walking by or getting out of a house. Then I got out of the car and casually walked toward the house, still checking, and then turned in at the walkway to the rear of the house where I knew she had her bedroom. I was right out of my skull. The windows were all dark, but I could hear them. They were in bed and he was talking to her wit his ugly sullen voice of his. I couldn't hear the words just the sound of his voice. I remembered all the beautiful things I had said to her in that bed, in that room, my voice filled with love and wanting. Then I heard her voice saying seductively, "Here let me help." Yeah, I could just imagine what she was helping him with. I had to get out of there before I lost what little sanity I had left. I tore myself from the window and passed by young Michael's stroller, remembering what I thought was a beautiful night with Christina and the next morning, with Michael happily on my shoulders as we explored the woods by Humber College. A happy rich day, gone now, gone forever, it was all gone.

I drove back to the boat, carefully. I was in a dangerous state of mind. When I got to the boat, I wrote and wrote. I had to get it out.

The next day I phoned Debbie, the lawyer who had helped Christine with her divorce and the restraining order on George, told her what had happened. She said, "Paul, she is dangerous. Christina is a very damaged girl who is not capable of any kind of relationship. She will not come back to you. Forget her or she will ruin your life. She can generate an incredible intensity of negative sexual energy and you have been exposed to too much of it already. She is a dark spirit, Paul, be careful."

I said, "You are right. She reminds me of Marilyn Monroe in Miller's, "After the Fall.""

"She is worse than Marilyn Monroe and speaking of that sexual energy field of hers, I'll tell you a story. A year ago, we were in the courthouse waiting for her case to come up. We were sitting out in this long hall. There was this guy sitting at the end of the hall. It must have been fifty yards away. She gives him the look. He gets up and walks the fifty yards up to her and starts chatting her up. I couldn't believe it.

Paul, forget her, gather your friends about you, go out to plays, movies, art galleries. Do things. Get her out of your system. Read F. Scott Fitzgerald's, <u>Tender is the Night.</u> Nichole doesn't get better and neither will Christina."

Debbie was, of course, right, and that was what I had to do. One of the plays I went to see was "The Grace of Mary Traverse." A line in it resonated within me, "She is one of the dark spirits of the world and everything she touches is ruined." That was Christina. With her I thought I was in the vale of Venus. Instead, I was lying in some dark place, ripped, torn and bleeding, in the shadow of the goddess. I remembered that night during the tea ceremony when her face changed before my eyes. Now I realized I was being warned, but I was too much in love to heed. She was so charming, beautiful and affectionate that I threw caution aside and took her into my heart.

Years later, I learned, through a mutual friend, that Mr. Punk Rocker had killed himself, that she was no longer beautiful and her children had turned out badly. They never had a chance and neither did I.

I was a long time healing. Christina was not my last dark goddess. Slowly 1 came to see that they are love's walking wounded. They are dangerous, often not wanting to be so, but dangerous, nevertheless. My last dark goddess declined my proposal of an intimate camping trip, saying, "No, Paul I know what I do." She had a conscience. I loved her and I still do, but her old wounds, her fear and her shadow make her dangerous.

But the question I needed to answer was why I am projecting my anima goddess onto these dangerous women. Why am I coming to them hoping for warmth and love? It is a doomed, Catch-22 trip, which leaves me ripped and torn, with my hopes and dreams in tatters. Why am I entrusting my hopes and dreams to these dark spirits? I had to find the answer.

CHAPTER FOUR

The Code: Prescription for Disaster

But I was not alone in my goddess trip. The media reports a steady stream of men lost in it and stalking, beating, even killing their partners. The most celebrated case was, of course, O.J. Simpson. Nichole was his goddess, and when she walked out of his life, all his hopes for joy, bliss and feeling life walked out with her. He was ripped, then enraged, murderously enraged, and she was going to pay for it. O.J. descended into the hell of the goddess meltdown.

With all the attention on that case, I was sure someone would intelligently explore the dynamics of this bad craziness, but no one did. The coverage never went beyond the depth of a super market tabloid. O.J.'s meltdown recalled a paragraph in Gay Hendricks,' <u>Conscious Loving,</u>

> Some of the most unhappy people...are those who resisted or delayed learning how to be their own persons... If you live your life through other people, you create a deep dependency that can backfire in a major way if they move away. When separation comes, you have no sense of self to sustain you. Facing life as an empty shell can be deeply troubling...

When O.J., in his white Bronco, was being pursued down the L.A. freeway by the California State Police, he was ready to kill himself. His friend talked him out of it. O.J. was, indeed, "deeply troubled." We men get ourselves into these "deeply troubled" states because we look to women to make us feel alive. We have "no strong sense of self to sustain us" because the male culture has failed to teach us how to create a self and a life.

Another man in a "deeply troubled" state was Constable Hotte. The Globe and Mail of November 28, 2002 had his story,

> An RCMP officer, Constable Jocelyn Hotte, accused of killing his ex-girl friend and wounding three of her male friends testified yesterday that he was in a trance like state when he riddled her car with bullets from his 9mm service pistol during a wild car chase in Montreal last year,
>
> "I had lost all control of myself. I wasn't myself. I wasn't in control of my emotions. It was like I was in the dark. I lost count of time. I lost contact with my surroundings. When I was firing, I didn't feel the trigger. I didn't smell the gunpowder... I was in an abnormal state of mind."

What a sad, grim tale. This poor devil never knew what happened to him. There he is in court, on trial for murder, his life in shambles, trying to explain to the court and to himself what had happened. in one over-powering moment. In the throws of his goddess projection over his ex-girlfriend, he had been free falling into some black hole deep within himself. Constable Hotte's testimony is very interesting because he reveals much of the inner state of mind during these times.

"How do we men get ourselves into these disastrous states of mind? How does it happen?" Asking that question took me in two directions: the male code and then Carl Jung's insights into the male psyche. First, the code: it's as if we men are all living in one huge fraternity house. The fraternity has a collective lore about manhood: what is it all about, how is it acquired, love, sex, women, relations with women, male identity, the superiority of men, in short,

"What is the right stuff." These questions are never directly addressed; it is all indirect. There is a whole store of history, tradition and institutions: all about manhood. This culture and lore teaches newly initiated members its answers to these questions. The house journals, Playboy and its clones, Maxim, Stuff, FHM, etc., pontificate monthly on these matters. All of this has a deep influence on the emerging psyche of a young man. But how real is this lore, how well does it prepare a man for the turbulent waters of life, love, sex and relationship?

Most of us are surprised to learn that boxing, professional wrestling, Playboy magazine, football, stock car racing even demolition derbies are all part of the culture and with huge attendance numbers and a high level of emotional involvement. Anthropologists define culture as, "a body of learned behavior common to a human society. It acts rather like a template which shapes consciousness even before behavior occurs." Culture has been compared to the water in which a fish swims. It goes largely unexamined. It is simply assumed that this is reality and this is the way things are. The water, in which men swim and have their lives, is filled with a wide range of beliefs, values and assumptions about life and what it is to be a man. This unexamined culture is all the more powerful precisely because it is unexamined and hence it will continue to be assumed. It will continue to be the modus operande for these men and it will affect behavior even before awareness and consciousness.

The roots of the word "culture" reveal its depth and power. The word comes from the Latin "cultus": to cultivate, to tend; hence, culture is that which cultivates us as we grow to maturity. It is deeper than intellect. It operates on a level suggested by the French phrase "bien dans sa peau" which literally translates: "how he is in his skin." The male culture teaches men "how to be in their skins."

But what is it teaching; car racing makes danger and risk taking into a manly virtue. Football, hockey, boxing and professional wrestling: all sports that teach that physical strength and prowess, aggression, the determination to win and, most of all, dominating the opponent, is the right stuff, and real men are ready to suffer pain or risk of injury for the sake of it.

Sports are huge in the fraternity, particularly physical contact team sports. They are the testing ground for the right stuff. Winning at these sports is very big in the fraternity. In the immortal words of Vince Lombardi, the great football coach, posted up in many of the locker rooms of North America, "Winning isn't everything, it's the only thing." Then, if you can't make it to the Super Bowl, there is corporate, financial, and political winning. Winners acquire and do those things, which will further attest to his manhood: the cars, the clothes, the cool, the resorts and finally the possession of a desirable, beautiful woman. The phrase "trophy wife" is no accident; that is what beautiful women are in the macho world. Sinatra's "Rat Pack" referred to women as "cuff links"-an accessory.

Very few men question the lore of the fraternity, which defines masculinity in these terms. The failure of the fraternity house culture is all around us. We now have a divorce rate of approximately fifty percent, which does not include those relationships, which have failed, but did not result in divorce. Therefore, the real success rate is well below fifty percent. The media continually report a sad stream of cases and statistics of domestic abuse, emotional and physical. Cultures with arranged marriages do better.

A man who understands nothing more than the lore will

find himself ill prepared for a relationship with a woman. Faced with the inevitable challenges and emotions involved in any relationship he resorts to the code: physical strength, domination, determination to win and the rest of the macho attributes, but this is not working. Clearly, something is very wrong.

Michael Paymar's, <u>Violent No More,</u> further reveals how wrong the code is. The book gives us a number of insights as to what drives these men who batter and abuse their women. Michael is training coordinator for the Duluth Domestic Abuse Intervention Project called by The New York Times, "the model for the rest of the country." His book contains case histories and personal accounts of a number of men who have battered their women. One of them, Jim, tells of his wife going to a high school football game, "She wasn't home when I thought she would be. I was in a total red rage and went out looking for her. When I came home and she was there." He describes how he beat her, then says, "I thought she had brought it on herself. I was convinced that she was out looking for another guy. The way I saw it, she shouldn't have been gone so long and she should have been home with me, case closed. I really believed she asked for it." He holds her responsible for his own feelings of need, insecurity and rage. "Case closed," he says, as he is totally convinced of his own inner logic. A number of men, like Jim, tell of feeling jealous and insecure after a party where there wives were having a good time, talking with other men and women or out with friends. This would trigger a torrent of verbal abuse insulting her looks, her sexuality, her person. Often, if she was going back to college or university, her efforts were viciously belittled. What emerges from these accounts is a concerted, determined campaign of verbal and physical abuse unconsciously designed to control and dominate the woman. The verbal abuse, the name calling, the insults, the degradation are all designed to strip the woman of her self esteem, her confidence and her spirit because deep down the abuser knows that a strong sense of selfhood will jeopardize his control over her.

These men feel jealous of their partner's friends, talents and ambitions, in short, any life of their own apart from him. Jealousy is a nasty mix of need, desire and insecurity. To these men, any interest, friend or activity of hers apart from him is a threat. Why are these men so insecure and vulnerable? Because they feel incomplete without her and they cannot bear it. Frank, from the Duluth Program, reflected back on his abusive relationship, "When I think back, I know I was dependent on women, emotionally, financially, sexually. I felt I needed a female counter partner in my life to make me whole. I had low self-esteem and a lack of love of myself. I was so jealous. If she hurts me, I'll hurt her back." "I'll hurt her back," he holds her responsible for his own inner torment. His fear of her leaving is so powerful that he compulsively believes that it must be true. One therapist calls this, "delusional jealousy."

The macho culture leaves a man so psychologically and spiritually impoverished that he is set up for this kind of jealousy and compulsive need around women. From there it is a short step to the abuse and violence we have seen in these cases.

When a friend, Debora, lent me her copy of Dr. William Pollack's, Real Boys, several major pieces dropped into place. In Real Boys, Pollack observes the early beginnings of the code and the depth of it in our society:

> I believe the trauma of separation is one of the earliest and most acute developmental experiences boys endure. An experience which plays a large role in the hardening process

through which society shames boys into suppressing their empathic and vulnerable sides.

Pollack is a professor of psychiatry at Harvard Medical School, and a Fellow of the Society for the Psychological Study of Men and Masculinity of the American Psychological Association. In this revealing work, he tells of five year old Johnny Martin starting kindergarten and throwing up every day in the wastebasket. On the very first day, he was uneasy and distressed, clinging to his mother. As the voice of the principal came over the loud speaker saying it was time for the parents to say good-bye, Johnny's mother was unsure and lingered. Pollack observed:

> Rachel, the teacher, offered the traditional prescription: "A clean break and he'll be OK." The mother whispered to Johnny, "Now, be a big boy not like your cry baby like your little sister and you'll be fine... But before she reached the door, Johnny began to cry with a wail that could be heard all the way down the hall to Mr. Bartlett, the school principal. In a flash, he was on the scene and called for Ms. Friedland, the school nurse. Ms. Friedland, a woman in her late fifties, came and advised that Rachel would need to be stricter with the students. "You'll learn, Rachel, that setting a firm limit is the best thing especially for boys!"
>
> When Rachel asked, "Why boys?" Ms. Friedland delivered a perfect summary of the Boy Code. "Separation is hard for girls," she explained with authority, "since they are so close to their mothers. Boys, however, have to be more independent or their peers will call them sissies and make fun of them. It's our job to help boys deal with this, especially if their mothers haven't done it themselves." She glanced at Johnny's mother. "You don't want Johnny to become over dependent do you?" she asked. "Let's see if we can get him to handle things on his own."
>
> Now the "experts" were involved, Johnny's mother was told that she could feel free to leave. Johnny was still crying as

Mom left. Later that week...I asked Rachel how things were going...

"What about Johnny Martin?"

"You'll see for yourself in a minute..."

The bell rang and almost all the parents scattered...when I turned around, I saw Johnny Martin, isolated from his classmates on the side of the room, vomiting into a small wastepaper basket.

"What's the matter, Rachel?' I asked.

"He's been doing that every day after his mother leaves, crying and throwing up!"

"What does the school nurse have to say?"

"Well, Ms. Friedland thinks he's over attached to his mother, that if this disruption continues, he may need a special class or therapeutic counselling."

As we spoke Johnny kept vomiting...There and then I broke a vow I had made to myself never to give a teacher advice when I was only invited to "observe" ...but Johnny was traumatized and Rachel, a novice at her job, but empathic at heart, knew something was wrong. I explained that vomiting was a stage two response to unbearable separation, an escalation from the crying that had led to no adequate response and next might come a more dangerous withdrawal. Then the nurse and principal would have a self-fulfilling prophecy of a "special needs" boy on their hands.

I told Rachel that all kids separate at their own rates and that boys need not be pushed to separate more quickly than girls... She breathed a sigh of relief, and when Ms. Friedland came to check in, Rachel told her that since the present plan was not working, and since it was her classroom, she would try a technique of her own. Johnny's mother was invited back and would stay until her child felt more comfortable and felt less pressure to separate.

A month later, I saw Rachel again. "Thanks for your advice," she said. "It worked wonderfully...after about ten days he let his mom leave without any fuss. Now if only I can get up the courage as a second year teacher to confront Mr. Bartlet and Ms. Friedland about this policy and the needs of the boys in my class, I'll be all set."

This is the Boy Code in action and these "professionals," a nurse and a school principal, have bought into it and advised a young teacher on the basis of it. These people have been trained in early childhood education. They should know better. This demonstrates how pervasive and widely believed the Code is through out our culture. Johnny Martin had a close call; he nearly suffered a wounding, which could have been with him a long, long time and all because of this absurd and wrong code. The nurse and the principal are not cruel people; they mean well, but they are deeply misinformed. They believe the Code is in the best interest of the boy; it is not.

A section of <u>Real Boys</u> is entitled: "Emotional Shaping In a Mother's Reactions: Infants Being Fitted For the First Gender Straitjacket." Here Pollack reports on the research of Haviland and Malatesta at Rutgers University. They found that male infants are much more emotionally expressive than girls are and that the mothers failed to empathize with or to recognize their son's negative emotional states. Instead, they urged their sons to stop crying, to smile and to "be a good boy." How many times have we heard that from a mother to her son? But these mothers were not insensitive or uncaring of their son's needs and feelings, they thought they were doing the right thing; they were unconsciously measuring their sons up against the Code. They were concerned that their sons were being too emotional, too easily upset, too weak and needy to be "real boys." But the subliminal message given to the boys was clear: having needs and being upset was not all right, they must be smile and be quiet. If you want approval, cut off your real feelings, conform and disconnect from your real self.

On the other hand, the daughters received far more

empathy and acceptance for their needs, distress and feeling upset. Haviland and Malatesta's research is more evidence of how deeply the Boy Code and its emotional straitjacket is ingrained into our culture. During the maturing and separation process, if a boy feels that his feelings are heard and respected, he will be reassured and able to move through it without trauma or wounding. But if he is forced and shamed into it, there will be scaring which he may carry into adolescence and possibility through out his entire life. Independence, like swimming, needs to be carefully taught. Throwing someone into the deep end of the pool is not the way.

The Code is based on a half truth that men need to mature out of their infantile dependence and their need of their mother, but the rest of that truth is that this must take place at a time and pace and in a way that feels secure and reassuring to us. The child's psyche is programmed to move out of that dependence. He will want to take little ventures out on his own. When my son, Jesse, was little, we would take him for walks in the park. Like most boys, he would occasionally run off on his own. We would follow at a discrete, careful distance sometimes hiding behind a tree or bush in order to give him his little adventure. Then when he needed us, we were there. It was OK, he was OK. He enjoyed these adventures; he knew he was learning how to be a big boy. Every little boy wants to become a "Big Boy." These little games build awareness, confidence and responsibility. They are fun and reassuring for both the parents and the children.

Boys, even more than girls, are internally programmed to achieve this sort of independence, but many mothers over protect their sons because of their own anxiety and insecurity, with the result they deny their boys this sort of maturing experience. They unconsciously communicate their own anxiety and insecurity to the child. Then when kindergarten or camp comes, the child is not prepared and they feel insecure, upset or even panic-stricken. This is not to say that every insecure boy is his mother's fault. Every child has his individual makeup and some have far more difficulty with this than others. Child rearing is a subtle art and every parent would do well to study the process and themselves in it very carefully. It is not easy, but when you are doing it right there is a precious connection and a trust with your child.

How many times have we heard a small boy say, "Let me do it!" Well, whenever possible, let him do it. Build his competence and confidence. Most boys love to play with their father's tools because they intuitively sense that tools are associated with masculine competence. With Jesse, I put some screws and a bolt into a board and showed Jesse how to use a screwdriver and a socket wrench. He loved it. Somewhere he knew his father was instructing him in the lore of manhood and it created a beautiful bond between us.

When Johnny Martin's mother said to him, "Now, be a big boy not like your cry baby little sister and you'll be fine," she was employing another article of the Boy Code: being masculine is rejecting the feminine; it is defined in the negative: not being a girl. Pollack observed a boxing match in an elementary school gym class. A boy made an awkward swing and the coach said, "Not like that, Michael, you're swinging like a girl." These people should know better; they should know how damaging something like that would be to a boy. They have been professionally trained as teachers. Once again we see how widely accepted the Code is in our culture. Boys are told to "act like a man," without really being taught what that means other than, "Don't be like a girl" or, "You're not good enough." Not at all helpful to a young boy trying to figure these things out.

Later on in high school, woe betide any boy who reads a poem or a dramatic part with any feeling. There will be snickers and whispered exchanges of "faggot." The code clearly states that the faintest trace of the feminine will not be tolerated. He will pay for it. Another bylaw of the Code: you build up your own virility by enforcing the Code and tearing other men down.

Pollack did a study he called, "Listening to Boy's Voices." One of the voices was Raphael, 17,

"Sometimes people say there are two me's, like I have a dual personality...The public persona is not really who I am. It's a tool... to be who everyone wants me to be."

Glenn, age 18,

"I'm always thinking: 'don't let your feelings show."

Ian, age 14,

"You've gotta really keep your guard up. If you don't, the guys will... tell people that you're not cool."

Jason, age fifteen, wrote:

"If something happens to you, you have to say: 'Yeah, no big deal,' even when you are really hurting....you have to punch things and brush it off. I've punched so many lockers in my life, it's not even funny. When I get home, I'll cry about it.

Adam told Pollack,

"I get a little down, but I'm very good at hiding it. It's like I wear a mask. Even when the kids call me names or taunt me, I never show them how much it crushes me inside. I keep it all in."

There it is, the code: "keep it all in," and woe onto those who break with the code because things will get even worse, many times worse. Those who are unable to maintain the Code are ruthlessly hounded and scapegoated. Pollack, in

"Voices", tells of a revealing scene between a small six-year-old boy and his mother. "It was a Little League game; Peter was at bat and had just been hit in the head with a pitch. His mother rushed out on the field to comfort her son. 'Not here, Mom,' she later told me he had whispered to her while stifling his tears. Peter, at seven years old, already knew that the code mandated that a public display of hurt and vulnerability was unacceptable-"Big guys don't cry on the field." He knows already at seven that "sucking it up," "gutting it out" and enduring the pain is the stuff of the code and he was in danger of shame and loss of face.

Enduring pain is very big in the code. The Los Angeles Times of January 6, 2001 reports:

> Scores of teenage boys from Los Angeles and neighboring counties come here every weekend to wrestle, using the moves they've learned on TV.
>
> Some of the more extreme teen wrestlers beat each other over the head with steel folding chairs and draw blood with baseball bats wrapped with barbed wire.... Backyard wrestling is one of the hottest sports for teen boys these days...
>
> An estimated 1000 federations have sprung up around the U.S. in the last two years... One of the boys, Chris Jackson, 19, said, "Yeah, sure, we're getting hit in the head with chairs and getting cut and everything, and bleeding, but, you know, we walk away." Another boy said, "Cuts heal, pain goes away... We're still none the less having fun." His stage name is Mr. Fantastik.
>
> Matt Heersink, 16, recently took at least four hard blows to the head with a steel-folding chair. That was after he'd been clobbered on his noggin a baseball bat, (then) he fell into a bale of barbed wire. "It was a great reaction from the crowd," says Matt, his head wrapped in a towel to sop up the blood, "That's what you're really looking for."

"Fun" is a curious word here, just what is it they are calling "fun"? What these boys are looking for from the crowd and from each other is the recognition and affirmation of their manhood. Backyard wrestling is more strange and bizarre stuff from the code. The film, "The Fight Club" was about the same twisted sense of masculinity, manhood as the capacity and willingness to endure pain. Many gang initiations involve the gang swarming on the initiate and beating him as though the violence and pain is some kind of test that will create a bond between those who inflict it and those who endure it.

Most hazing is a variation on this theme. The code can take strange, bizarre, even horrific twists. In its darkest reaches, the code equates a capacity for violence with manhood. Last year in Toronto a gang of boys swarmed on a boy, they did not know, and beat and kicked him to death. (This stuff is getting very tough to write. I haven't touched my typewriter in a week.) At their trial, Toronto, June 2, 2003, Yaviore Lipschitz testified,

> "I know that Meir, lee, and Dan kicked...Dmitri...like a rag doll." (Meir Mariani, William "Lee" Cochrane, both 20, and Daniel Weiz, 22, the three young men charged in Baranovski's death) "He was not defending himself. He was getting kicked around like a lifeless bag... He was gasping for his life. He lifted his head and made an awful noise and then Meir gave him a swift Soccer kick...His neck went back and he didn't move after that."

We will never know exactly what was going on in their minds as they were kicking that boy to death, but Lipschitz gave up a few clues as he continued, "Running out of the park, we just started bragging, said stupid things...Just giving each other fives and saying, "Good kicks. "Lipschitz claimed he didn't participate in the attack, but boasted with his friends because "I was trying to make a rep for myself...a rep as a bad ass."

"A rep...as a bad ass," this is the stuff of masculinity and identity with these young men. This is their idea of the "right stuff." What a nightmare. This is no isolated incident. This attitude toward violence, holding it as some kind of proof of masculinity is seen all too often.

Shame is essential to understanding the code and its quest for manhood. Shame is nothing less than a diminishment of our selfhood, our being, which to a boy and a man is one with his masculinity. In the ghetto "hood", the word for it is "dissed," a contraction of disrespected. Boys are shot and killed for "dissing." This is serious stuff. Any insult to their fragile selfhood is an explosive issue and guns, knives and violent retribution become the way to restore that shaky manhood.

The US Secret Service studied the boys who shot teachers and classmates in Columbine, Colorado and other schools and they found that these boys were loners and outsiders who had been hounded, taunted and tormented by their classmates. Since Columbine, there have been a number of similar shootings by male high school students with similar profiles. They had been found wanting by the Code and were ruthlessly punished and shamed and they snapped under the strain. They were crushed by the Code and they went berserk under the pain, humiliation and loss of selfhood. One investigator said, "These boys were crying with bullets." The code is an ugly business; it is time to see the Code for what it is: a cruel and dangerous definition of manhood. The wounds inflicted by the Code and its abrupt disconnection can fester in the psyche and produce real horror. A Japanese serial rapist and killer, Joji Obara wrote in his journal: "To take revenge on the world I will have to become a villain."

Those boys at Columbine appear to have been on the same principle. They killed themselves after taking some of that revenge first.

Pollack writes, "While girls may be shame sensitive, boys are shame phobic...they fear it... they are exquisitely yet unconsciously attuned to any signal of "loss of face" (or "dissing") and will do just about whatever it takes to avoid shame." Understanding shame is essential here. Shame is a denial or an insult to one's selfhood, hence, one's manhood.

Growing up with the Code leaves a man disconnected and disassociated from his feeling self. He does not seek that kind of connection with others nor does he does he give it. He believes that feeling and connection is a threat to his masculinity. His own feelings of vulnerability, any fear, doubt, insecurity, need, are a threat to his masculinity. They raise doubt as to whether or not he has the "right stuff" and not having that is the ultimate defeat. Tom Wolfe nailed it with his book by that name about the fighter pilots in the astronaut program. Their studied bravado, drinking and driving, the Corvettes, the wild capers, the risk taking, all textbook responses to the Code and the continual effort to prove ones self worthy according to it.

The Code demands this hardening process. Everything outside the Code is repressed and thrown down into the basement, which is the unconscious, and the door dropped down on it. But these needs, the need for this kind of intimacy and connection does not go away and locked away down in the basement it grows and grows so that when we are grown men we are perfect candidates for the Goddess Projection. The Goddess, who with her magical powers can make all this right; if only she will. If only I can win her and have her.

But it does not have to be like this. I remember when my

son, Jesse, was four. We were out on my sailboat, Wizard, when I ran aground on a sandbar just off the Ward's Island landing. The Queen City Yacht Club launch came by and offered to tow me off if I came on board his boat to tend the line so it would not foul up in his prop. I explained to Jesse what I had to do. He said, "I will be afraid." I tried to reassure him that he will be all right and that I will be right back. But as soon as I stepped off the boat, he began to cry. We soon pulled Wizard off the sand bar. I jumped back on board Wizard, picked up Jesse, held him tight and told him that I was sorry that I had to do that and make him feel bad.

In other words, it was OK for him to have those feelings. It was OK to cry. The Code would have had me say something like, "Stop your crying and be a big boy. You got nothing to cry about. What are you some kind of little sissy?" and the message, loud and clear, would have been, "It's not OK for you to have these feelings and even worse to express them. It is not the stuff of manhood; it's not the right stuff."

This coming from the most important male figure in his life would have been crushing. Well, today Jesse is very solid, assured, masculine, twenty- four year old, young man. Breaking with the code, did not hurt him one bit.

Professor Robyn Fivush at Emory University found that parents when guiding their sons through conflicts encouraged anger and retaliation, "Anger is the OK emotion," While with their daughters they favored re-establishing harmony as the solution. Professor Don Long of Washington University calls anger the "emotional funnel" through which boys have been taught to express their feelings of frustration, vulnerability and powerlessness. The more tender and real emotions, the ones more close to the bone are too shameful to show. So anger becomes the OK emotion for men to express and their quickest response to a difficult situation, hardly the best preparation for close relationships.

Fathers are often deeply involved in the Code. Robert Duval in the film, "The Great Santini," plays a macho Marine fighter pilot, who taunts and shames his adolescent son about his manhood. At one point, he suggests his son is wearing a training bra. The son is on the school basketball team. During a game, Santini goes nearly berserk, when his son is fouled and knocked down by an opponent. Santini raves at his son: "Get him...You better get him, goddamnit, or don't come home." The son deliberately fouls his opponent back and is kicked out of an important game. The coach is furious, but the son knew he just had to do it. You see this kind of involvement at Little League hockey, baseball and football games where the son's masculinity reflects on the father and he cannot tolerate any possible failure to measure up to the Code.

Fathers will use language on their sons that they would never use on their daughters like, "you disgust me" or teasing with something like, "you ding-a-ling." These fathers think that by humiliating their sons they will make them into men. A CBC documentary on junior league hockey caught a mother on tape mercilessly shaming her eleven-year-old son for missing a body check and letting an opponent score. She hammered him saying over and over, "You don't even want to know what I'm thinking." The kid was crushed; it was brutal.

In Reading, Massachusetts, July 5, 2000, Thomas Junta, beat to death, Michael Costin, father of a twelve-year-old hockey player who was opposing his son in a game. Junta's own self hood was so closely identified with his son's that he lost contact with reality and killed a man, ruined his own life and scarred his son's forever. Selfhood is a life and death issue. The thinking and understanding of these parents of how their boy comes to be a man is that wrong. These parents, no doubt, think that they are toughening their sons up and making them more masculine with this shaming and taunting and demands for better and better performance, but they have a personal involvement as they push their sons to live up to the Code. All this puts tremendous pressure on a young impressionable boy and sends him a message, which is not going to help him one bit in his struggle for manhood. It pushes him into an emotional straitjacket which he may wear the rest of his life. It may keep him from living a full emotional life and diminish his ability to enter into an intimate relationship with another. <u>Obsessive Love</u> quotes a patient, Robert,

> Nothing I ever did was good enough for him. I was never good enough for him. If I left a book out on my desk, I'd get a lecture about a being a slob. If I brought home anything less than straight "A's", I'd get a lecture on how I wasn't trying hard enough. If I dropped a pop fly, I'd get a lecture on how I wasn't trying hard enough. On those rare occasions when I did something right, he'd say, "It's about time." I always felt like he didn't want me because I wasn't the son he thought he deserved.

A young boy cannot understand that his father's standards are unreasonable. We feel that we are failures. The psychological damage from this kind of denigrating abuse from our fathers is damaging beyond calculation. When Robert was rejected by his lover he became so enraged that he smashed her car and got himself into considerable difficulty. Robert's situation with his father is an extreme case, but even the typical conflict that most families have over school, grades and homework can become a very difficult area requiring care and communication in order not to inflict similar damage. John Steinbeck did it right. When his son wanted to drop out of high school, he said to his son "I know a lot of your teachers are dullards who do not know anything and should not be teaching. But if you drop out you will miss out on the few who are fine inspiring teachers and I would hate to see you miss out on what they could give you." This kind of straight talk, compassionate, real and loving, can work wonders and it did here. Steinbeck reached his son and he went back to school.

Toeing the mark in the system, in school or at work, is not easy for anyone especially for an adolescent boy, but we, as parents, know the heavy price taken for not paying your dues to the establishment. We love our sons and do not want to see them pay this price, but many fathers don't know how to communicate their love to their sons. The love does not come through; what comes through instead is the unspoken message, "I'm not happy with you," "You're not good enough," "You are rejected," then the son, to save himself from this kind of diminishment and pain, distances himself from his father. The father feels the separation and bores in with more demands and criticism with the result the relationship between them deteriorates even more.

Another by-law of the Code states that we prove our masculinity with our willingness to take risks. In today's Toronto Star, March 10, 2001, is an account of three teenage boys from Pouch Cove, Newfoundland who drowned while playing a game of "Copying", a game of follow the leader as he jumps from one ice flow to the next as the ice is breaking up in the town's harbour. If you are "chicken," afraid to run the risk, you do not have the "right stuff." Adolescent boys are running the risks every weekend in automobiles and motorcycles with tragic results.

When I was in the Air Force taking flight training, a guy

named Nixon had the unofficial record for the number of turns, sixteen, in a spin for the T-28, hence, his nickname, Spinner. The standard number of turns for the manoeuvre was three. Sixteen turns meant a major loss of altitude and a high rate of descent. One day Spinner went up to break his record. After he was two hours overdue with no radio contact, they sent out search planes. They found him in a hole in the desert. There wasn't a piece of his aircraft much bigger than a playing card. They figured he went into the ground in excess of 300 Knots. He left behind a young wife with a one-year-old boy. What was he doing up there? He was proving his manhood by pushing the envelope beyond what anyone else has done. He was listening to the Macho Code. Being a husband and a father wasn't enough; it didn't register with the Code. He had to be the top guy, another by-law of the code.

Pollack speaks of the straightjacket of the "Boy Code" with its false machismo, a code, which has failed its believers. The suicide rate for adolescent boys ages 15 to 19 has tripled since 1970. The Blackboard Jungle well names our schools. They are crucibles where the boy code is played out and woe betide any who are found wanting. The bullying, the fights, the guns, the gangs, it is all boys desperately asserting their manhood and their selfhood. The great psychoanalyst, Eric Erickson, believes that during adolescence a boy must form a coherent identity or else fall prey to a sense of despair and confusion. The adult models of manhood about us are not reassuring. Often we see our fathers shackled to a meaningless job that he hates and which drains him of life and vitality so we turn to fantasies of playing professional sports, driving race cars and the like for our male role models, or we turn to the violent characterizations on television and movies or to the code of the peer group and the gangs. But the "coherent identity" of which Erickson speaks is an urgent need which if frustrated can seek unreal and ugly channels.

The Boy Code works on us on two fronts: our parents and teachers on one side, our peers on the other. All of them convinced of the validity and necessity of this image of masculinity. The Boy Code becomes the Man's Code. Living the code leaves us wounded in the deepest reaches of our psyche. It leaves us disassociated from our feeling self and separated from the feminine qualities and energies of life. With the emptiness from this hardening process, we become prime candidates for an anima projection and a dependent, obsessive relationship with a woman, in extreme cases, a violent, sometimes even deadly one. This is the legacy of the boy code.

CHAPTER FIVE

Macho Man, Jung and the Goddess

In Chapter Four, I asked, "How do we men get ourselves into these disastrous states of mind? We have looked at the:code, now we look at Jung and his insights into the psyche. We have looked at the code, now we look at Jung.

The great Swiss psychologist, Carl Jung, saw that we all, men and woman, have a masculine and a feminine side to our psyches. Both are essential to our selfhood. Jung named the male feminine component, the Anima, which is Latin for soul and breath. An apt name, as both, breath and the feminine are subtle and most essential. Most of us men do not understand what feminine means. We think it means painting our bedrooms pink and hanging lace curtains. In <u>We: Understanding the Psychology of Romantic Love,</u> Robert Johnson writes:

> Feminine in this sense, does not mean, "Pertaining to women" but refers to inner, psychological qualities that are found in both men and women. When a man develops the strengths of his inner feminine, it actually completes his maleness as he becomes more fully human. Jung called this totality of the person, the self.

Jung wrote, "A man, therefore, has in him a feminine side, an unconscious feminine figure   a fact he is generally quite unaware.... I have called this figure, the anima"(CW 9,i, p512)...."every man carries Eve, his wife, hidden in his body." (CW 18, p429) Later Jung writes of the Anima "as having an extraordinary fascination...at a certain level, therefore, woman appears as the true carrier of the longed for wholeness and redemption." (CW 14, p500)

Jung sees the male psyche as preponderantly male, but with a recessive and unconscious feminine component, which cannot be ignored if the psyche is to be balanced, healthy and whole. Jung is saying that the Anima is essential to totality of every man's self, his person, his identity. Hence, soul making or the completion of the self inevitably involves the anima and the feminine.

But the psyche is driven to complete itself and seek fulfillment. When a man's Anima is stunted or neglected for any reason, he will be driven to find and fulfill that stunted part of himself in someway or another. When I was a toddler, displaced by my brother in my mother's attention and affection, the pain of my love for her was too great so I shut it down, but along with that pain all the rest of my feelings got shut down as well. I had shut down a major part of myself, my feeling self, which is the realm of my feminine. I shut down my first connection with the Divine Feminine. I shut down my young, still budding, Anima.

In my case, and this is by no means rare, I created a goddess in my unconscious who could give me everything I had not had. She would be the mother I always wanted, always hoped for. She would complete me. Joseph Campbell said, "We seek not the meaning of life, but the feeling of being fully alive. It is not meaning, that we seek, but unity and connection."

To be fully alive is a peak and wondrous experience, which we all seek in a myriad of different ways, but illusions and fantasies will not serve. Fulfillment will accept no substitutes. When we complete and fulfill ourselves, we have this wondrous experience of being fully alive. The goddess in my unconscious and in that of many men was an apparition, a shade, which seemed to possess the magical power to complete my life. She would restore my feeling life. I was in search of her and I would go to the ends of the earth for her. I would project her image onto one woman after another, one dysfunctional relationship after another.

We men are particularly vulnerable to this projection because our sexual partner is the same sex as our mother with the result that the two images in our unconscious become superimposed, one over the other, creating a single image of great power. When Jung spoke of the Anima "as having an extraordinary fascination" and appearing "as the true carrier of the longed for wholeness and redemption," he was speaking of the projected Anima.

That is why I was so devastated after Eileen and Christina. I had lost my goddess. When I was with her and she was loving me, I felt more alive than I had ever been before in my life. It was an illusion, of course, but a very, very powerful illusion. It was "love potion number nine," and it was the most powerful narcotic imaginable and I have been addicted to it for a long time. The Anima Projection is a very powerful dynamic. Jung's statement concerning the Anima is to be taken most seriously because when we project our Anima image onto a woman we will desperately need and want her. So much so that we can become very nearly insane with the power of these feelings. Christina was the heaviest trip of all. With her, I was as close to the edge as I ever want to go.

Jung is clear on this: we men must cultivate our feminine if we are to be whole, but how do we do this? First, we must ask the question, what is the feminine? The Greeks, with their mythology of six goddesses, Aphrodite, Athena, Demeter, Artemis, Hera and Persephone, have defined the feminine perhaps more fully than any other culture. Each goddess personifies one aspect of the feminine. Most of these have been savaged by the patriarchal culture, but it is Aphrodite who horrifies the patriarchy the most.

"The beautiful and venerable goddess who, all around Her, and beneath her light feet, causes the grass to grow."

Hesiod

"She causes the grass to grow" and flowers as well. Flowers and gardens express the sensuality of a culture. Flowers are the beautiful sexual organs of plants and are associated with the feminine. The fragrance of flowers and the perfume of women are all the realm of Aphrodite. She is, in all things, a sensuous presence. To the ancient Greeks she was "the golden goddess." Like a glorious sun, she shone down their precocious culture and blessed it with the arts of sculpture, poetry and music. Nothing delights her more than the gratification of the senses by beautiful means. She loves fine dresses, lustrous flowing hair, jewellery, adornments of all kinds...Today she rules the fashion industry, cosmetics, and the richly glamorous world of magazines such as Vogue...

To be blessed by Aphrodite means that a woman will be very much at ease with her body and have a healthy, uncomplicated relationship with her sexuality.

The Goddess Within - Jennifer and Roger J. Woolger

She is associated with gold, jewellery and fine clothing. She loves laughter, games, sweetness, men and relationship. She is the mother of Eros. For the Greeks, sexuality is a sacred gift and that is why they honored Aphrodite.

When Odysseus returns home to Penelope, they retire to her bed, "to honor their rituals." Rituals is the last word the macho sensibility would associate with sex. But between the Greeks and us stands Christianity, a religion whose early founders were horrified by Aphrodite's liberal love of the body and of sexual pleasure. Here is Gregory the Great on women and love, "The sirens have the faces of women, because nothing estranges men from God as much as the love of women." Origen, an early theologian, castrated himself thinking it would bring him closer to God. Once again, Jennifer and Roger Woolger,

> The psychological consequences of denying Aphrodite any real place in the culture of the later middle Ages were twofold: widespread sexual neurosis and the paranoia about witches....
>
> It is not generally known that the cult of the Virgin Mary was directly derived from the troubadours of the twelfth century. The Church feared that the troubadours' liberated view of women would undermine its priestly, and male, authority. Therefore, in the aftermath of the Albigensian Crusade (1209-1220) it took the opportunity to tar the troubadours with the same brush as the heretics. At the same time, it assimilated the worship of the individual lady of the troubadour cult to the worship of Our Lady, the Virgin...

Understanding the feminine is not easy especially from our Judeo Christian patriarchal culture whose only model is Mary, the Virgin Mother of God, a distant ethereal and unearthly figure of whom we know little. Jung sees replacing real women with the worship of Mary as a major setback for men's psychological development.It also distracts attention from the virtues of real women and femininity. However, there is an even grimmer consequence for this repression: the awakening in men's unconscious of the witch archetype. The Woolger's quote Jung on this,

> The relative depreciation of the real woman is compensated by demonic impulses (from the unconscious, which reappear) projected upon the object ...hence, she

appears as a persecutor, i.e. a witch. Thus the delusion about witches, that in eradicable blot upon the Later Middle Ages, developed along with, and indeed as a result of, the intensified worship of the Virgin.

Carl Jung has described how the loss of the troubadour's service to love and Aphrodite led to the witch-hunts. In a word, by substituting the worship of Mary, Aphrodite was driven underground, and her vilified image kept obsessively alive in the sadistic imaginings of the Inquisitors:

> Witches were believed to take part in orgies with the devil, with whom they performed every imaginable sexual act...these stories were all derived from "confessions" wrung from innocent women under appalling torture supervised by the male celibate priesthood of the time. Clearly, in psychological terms, the priests projected all their repressed and lurid sexual fantasies onto women and then punished them for it often with humiliating sexual torture. (See Norman Cohn's Europe's Inner Demons) Not even the racial crimes of the Nazis quite equal the depths of sexual hatred to which the so-called spiritual leaders of the late middle Ages sank.

This is the stuff of nightmares. Gordon Rattray Taylor states the unvarnished truth in <u>Sex in Society</u>, "It is hardly too much to say medieval Europe came to resemble a vast insane asylum." Yes, and with the worst of the lunatics in charge of the asylum. The contemporary church is paying the price of its fear and hatred of women, rejection of femininity and sexuality with the current scandal and horror of pedophile priests.

The ancient Greek representation of the feminine with their six goddesses is very useful because the feminine has many sides. Aphrodite is hardly the only side of the feminine. There is Hera, the Goddess of marriage, home monogamy and fidelity. She was the wife of Zeus, a stormy marriage, but she was happy to be the queen of Mount Olympus. The Hera woman is confident, in command of herself and others with a natural authority and presence, often from the social position as the wife of a successful, influential man. She sees herself as the essential woman behind the successful man. She enjoys the power of that position. Family, community, respectability and social position are very important to her. Marriage is the politics of partnership. A modern version of Hera was Nancy Reagan. Donald Regan writes of her in For the Record.

> Mrs. Reagan regarded herself as the President's alter ego not only in the conjugal but also in the political and official dimensions, as if the office that had been bestowed upon her husband somehow fell into the category of worldly goods covered by the marriage vows.

Hera is determined to be a player in the affairs of the community and of the world. Hillery Clinton is another modern Hera. The Heras of the world have been at the leading edge of women's rights and equality and often have suffered greatly for it. As in the sad case of the Puritan wife, Anne Hutchinson (1591-1643), an early American colonial settler reported in The Goddess Within:

> Hera's ambitions are seen as a threat to patriarchal supremacy and are curtailed, often brutally. Anne educated herself in the theology of her church, that of John Calvin, and had begun to challenge certain dogmas, encouraging women to discuss divine matters among themselves. She was tried for heresy, a charge never proven. The words of her condemnation by the Calvinist church fathers reveal how deeply women's power was feared and resented then: she was accused of being a "husband rather than a wife, a preacher rather than a hearer, and a magistrate rather than a subject." She was then driven from the Massachusetts Bay Colony and

died shortly afterwards, murdered by hostile Indians near New York.

Hera is a side of the feminine in sharp contrast to Aphrodite. Aphrodite's sensuality, her sexuality, her disregard for fidelity and monogamous marriage are all a threat to the stability and family life, which is so important to Hera. However, if she is to be wife to her husband, she must give him something of Aphrodite's allure and love of men. Aphrodite possessed a magic girdle with which she could seduce any man. At one, point Hera borrowed it from Aphrodite.

One comes away from a study of these goddesses seeing that every woman possesses a unique blend of these qualities, hopefully, a harmonious blend, which describes the several aspects of her femininity. This is not a simple piece of work as some of these contradict each other, as do Aphrodite and Hera. The other four of Greek mythology are Artemis, Demeter, Persephone and Athena.

Artemis is a beautiful huntress with bow and arrow living alone in the wild. She has little use for the domestication of Hera nor the gowns and jewellery of Aphrodite. She is physical and energetic, always out of doors. There is a tomboy quality about her. She has an animal energy about her, which can be quite sensual, but her sexuality is quite different from Aphrodite's. She may take a man, who attracts her and shares her love of the wild, her adventures and her energetic life, but she will not give up her independence and there will be none of the togetherness of Hera's domestic life.

Artemis is the goddess of wild nature, she haunts the woods, the groves, the luscious meadows...She protects and fosters the young of animals and growing human children. She is the Mistress of Animals," a woman holding in her hands four-footed animals or birds of different kinds.

<u>A History of Greek Religion</u>   Martin Nilsson

I know of one young Artemis who refuses to wear dresses, anything pink or yellow, or anything with flowers on it. She loves horses, animals, and being out of doors. She is strong, beautiful and full of physical energy, a perfect Artemis.

In marked contrast to Artemis is Athena, she is extroverted, intelligent, practical, and worldly. She is interested in people, ideas, and business. She enjoys the bustle of the market place and the action of politics. She was born, full grown, arrayed in her armor and with sword, as she came forth from the very forehead of Zeus to be the friend and companion to great warriors in battle. She played a major role in the Trojan War. She is a long way from Aphrodite. In all of this, the modern Athena can seem a rival and a threat to men.

Persephone is goddess of the underworld. Dragged down to the Underworld by Hades, she reins there as Queen. A few hundred years ago, she could have been one of the medieval mystics. In our time, her nature could be defined by the prefixes para, Meta and super. Her world is metaphysics, the supernatural and parapsychology beyond the physical and the natural. She has a sense of these things and looks for the deeper levels of reality. To describe her life's path, the Woolger's quote T.S. Eliot's "The Cocktail Party" where the psychiatrist counsels a young woman:

> (This way is unknown, and so requires faith)
> The kind of faith that issues from despair
> The destination cannot be described:

You will know very little until you get there
You will journey blind. But the way leads towards
                                        Possession
Of what you have sought for in the wrong place.

There is a mystical quality to this young woman and the psychiatrist recognizes the Persephone in her.

Demeter is the mother of us all. She is beyond just caring for her own, but reaches out to all that is young, needy, tiny or helpless. She is the archetypal mother. Several other goddesses can be mothers in their way, but with Demeter, mothering is her natural first instinct. She has little concern for anything else. She is not going canoeing, like Artemis, or involving herself in some romantic affair, like Aphrodite, nor will she be running for political office, like Athena, or redecorating the house, like Hera, nor leading a meditation group like Persephone. No, she is far too busy with her children's meals, clothing, activities, school and medicines when they are sick.

On the larger scale, she is the nurturer and the Great Mother. In ancient times, she had dominion over all forms of reproduction and the renewal of life. Her symbols are a sheaf of wheat and a single ear of corn, symbols of fecundity and of the fruit of the earth. According to Homer's Hymn to Demeter, she is tall, radiantly beautiful, "slim ankled and "golden haired" (like the corn she holds in her hand). She is granddaughter of Gaia, the Earth Mother and shares her concern and dominion of earth and nature. Demeter totally accepts her elder's earthy wisdom and consciousness. Demeter has suffered deeply from the patriarchy. Zeus plotted with his brother, Hades, the Dark Lord, to let him carry off her daughter, Kore, to the Underworld.

The Woolger's are right on entitling their book, not The

Goddess Within Women but simply, <u>The Goddess Within</u>, within us all, but the patriarchal culture has denied and ravaged many of these aspects of the feminine. We have done deep hurt to Aphrodite, Artemis, Persephone and especially to Demeter. These are the goddesses, which are closest to the mystery of the life force and of being itself.

Jacques Maritian, in Education at the Crossroads, writes of a deep attribute of the feminine,

> ...a simplicity and openness with regard to existence...(an) attitude of a being who *exists* gladly, is unashamed of existing, stands upright in existence, and for whom to be and to accept the natural limitations of existence are matters of equally simple assent. Trees and animals are like this.

We men need to assimilate this from the feminine- "to exist gladly" as we accept "the natural limitations of existence." The Hopi Indians have a word, "Koyaanisqatsi" which loosely translates, "life in turmoil, life out of balance," which well describes our patriarchal culture, with its continual threat of violence and warfare, its corruption, poverty-stricken peoples, massive arms expenditures and serious insult to the environment. It is sick because it is out of harmony with itself. What is missing is the feminine dimension in our psychic lives: a deep, mystical sense of the earth and her cycles and of the very cosmos as a living and sacred mystery. We have lost our inner connection to that momentous power that used to be called the Great Mother of us all. In the words of E.O. James, "she was the embodiment of creative power in all its fullness." Losing and even denying connection with powers of this magnitude has serious consequences.

CHAPTER SIX

The Problem of Beauty and Our Denial of the Feminine

On July 27, 1999, ABC's 20/20, reported the case of Andy Cook from Macon, Georgia. One night, Andy drove out to his favorite fishing spot on the shore of a nearby lake. It was also a local lover's lane. As Andy pulled up in his pick up truck, he saw a car parked there. He took his 9 mm automatic pistol and assault rifle out of his truck and riddled the car with bullets killing the couple inside. He never talked to them, hardly even saw them.

Eventually, Andy confessed to his father, an FBI agent. His father asked Andy why he did it. Andy couldn't tell him; he didn't know why. It was as mysterious to him as it is to everyone else. How could an otherwise O.K. person do this? Andy was in the grip of some deep unconscious force totally beyond his awareness. All we know of him is that he was a bit of a loner raised by a loving father after his mother left the family, but the fact that he carried a loaded M-16 and a Browning automatic pistol in his pick up truck says something about him.

On that 20/20 program father and son talked to each other, each mystified, stunned and anguished by this nightmare. Andy was no monster. I speak of him in the past tense, because he is now on death row, a dead man walking. We can only speculate on what went on inside Andy Cook's mind that night. He was familiar with the area so he must have known that this spot was a lover's lane at night, and perhaps he felt that what was going on inside the car was something he was not getting and had no prospects of getting. Perhaps Andy's alienation and emptiness welled up inside him and the pain and rage from that isolation totally overwhelmed him. A lightning bolt of blinding, overpowering emotion flashed through his psyche. In that moment, he destroyed their lives and his own, in a blind moment of which he has no understanding.

Andy Cook resembles a sad young man in James Joyce's short story, "A Painful Case," whom he describes as "an outcast from life's feast." John Bradshaw, in Creating Love In Your Life, quotes Carl Jung, "Any part of us that we do not accept unconditionally, splits off and becomes more and more primitive," he then quotes Virgina Sapier, "It becomes like a hungry dog in the basement." A dog growing hungrier and hungrier, more and more primitive.

If this feminine component, the anima, is rejected, ignored, then thrown down into the basement, it will become like this hungry, mean dog waiting for its time. This flash of blinding emotion raging through Andy's psyche may have been that hungry dog in the basement. The Course in Miracles says, "The journey into darkness has been long and cruel" and Andy Cook had gone deep into it. The macho code of Playboy magazine, the NFL, the National Rifle Association and the boy code, has totally failed Andy Cook, failed to prepare him for the turbulent water of a man's life journey. They gave him a model of masculinity, which left him totally unprepared to create and acquire the love, beauty, and relationship he desperately needed in his life. The Code made Andy Cook and countless other men, "outcasts from life's feast." The male culture has failed men with its rejection of the feminine. To deny the feminine is to deny the completion of the self. Then the stunted self blindly and destructively lashes out in some way, usually unconscious. The macho culture ignores fundamental needs of a man's psyche, and it left Andy Cook alone and abandoned in the male wilderness at the mercy of forces beyond his knowing, beyond his control. Andy Cook is not alone.

We men have little idea of how to cultivate the feminine. The male culture has failed to teach us how to proceed with this essential undertaking. Fortunately, I have Andrea, who instructs me in this ephemeral, but necessary quality. Yesterday, we were out in her garden and she brought out from the house a wide bowl half filled with water and placed it on a tree stump. "Pick out a few flowers and whatever else strikes you as beautiful." I picked three small yellow flowers and floated them on the surface of the water. Then I saw a bush with smoky purplish green leaves and I floated four of these on the water, then with four more purple flowers. It was good and seemed complete. Andrea instructed me to fully observe this lovely composition, I had created. I slowly let this soft, subtle, quiet and joyful beauty come to me, to let it speak to me and to connect with me. I was connecting with nature and beauty, the feminine and love. Women do this sort of thing and men almost never do. It is not in the code, and it leaves us starved for this congress with beauty and the feminine, which our soul craves.

The other day I was helping Linda, Jesse's mother move. She had a large planter filled with earth and a bulb the size of my fist. Growing off the bulb was a tangle of curled white roots reaching down into the brown earth. "There it is," I said, "the feminine, enmeshed into nature and the earth, at one with it, proceeding out of it." I knew I needed to garden, to plant into the earth, to tend it and watch it grow. Linda does this in spite of her painfully busy and demanding life, because it is essential to her. There is something profoundly beautiful and feminine about a woman tending her garden, picking off the dead leaves and flowers, cultivating the soil, watering, caring for the life and the potential beauty there, then waiting for that life to come forth.

A Stihl chainsaw poster portrays the dynamic between the shadow male and the feminine. We see a profoundly beautiful, untouched West Coast rain forest with giant sequoia trees. At the base of two of the trees are loggers with chain saws cutting into the trunks of the ancient trees. The copy in black capitals printed over the deep green of the forest canopy reads, "We came, We saw, We conquered."

This is how "real men" relate to pristine nature, mowing it down, conquering it with our strength, our tools and masculine skill. This is their idea of a connection with nature. This is what nature is for, to be taken, to be used, to be raped. Never let be for its own sake. David Suzuki did a series called "Planet For the Taking," for the CBC. This is what is going on around us every day as the hypermasculine takes the realm of nature for its own use and anyone who objects is contemptuously called "a tree hugger" or a "bleeding heart."

contemptuously called "a tree hugger" or a "bleeding heart."

Like President Reagan said, "You've seen one tree, you've seen them all," or in other words, "What's the big deal? No sense letting these or in other words, "What's the big deal? No sense letting these trees, these wilderness areas, shore lines, whatever, get in the way of some real money." That is the macho male talking and it is a denial and a rejection of the feminine love and concern for nature and the wild. This is a rape of Artemis and Demeter. Many men go to nature to hunt or to fish. The code allows for that; that's O.K. Saul Bellow, in <u>The Rain King</u>, says of hunting, "It's a strange way to relate to nature." This kind of violence to the feminine on the outer planes always has its source on the inner planes of the psyche.

My landlord, an old thoroughbred horse breeder, quite well off really, but he would not put any effort or attention to the house and grounds. He would say, "There is no money in it." He needed someone to say to him, "it's not about money," but he was a cranky old boy and he thought he had it all figured out. We men need to have flowers about, to cook good meals for ourselves and keep our houses looking like we were expecting a lady friend to come by. The lady friend is our own Anima, our own self. We need to court her like a lady, of whom we are quite fond, because if we do not fulfill these needs in ourselves, the needs of our Anima, then that need becomes externalized and projected onto some woman.

The feminine understands the profound value of deep and intimate relationship. The feminine understands that intimacy is worth the surrender of power it required to make the connection with another. The patriarchal male cannot surrender to the relationship and to the other. He must retain control with the result that he never fully enters the relationship and so he never achieves the connection with another person. He never receives the love that he seeks. The starved psyche desperately reaches out for congress with the feminine. The beauty of woman becomes a living symbol of the fullness of life and joy, which has eluded us. A symbol in our mind contemptuously called "a tree hugger" or a "bleeding heart."

Like President Reagan said, "You've seen one tree, you've seen them all," or in other words, "What's the big deal? No sense letting these A symbol, which takes on mythic proportions and can overwhelm the psyche. This is how the beauty of one woman can become an obsession and then we must have her. The Anima is Latin for soul and breath. Breath, a quiet and subtle thing, often taken for granted, but most essential. A drowning man struggling for breath is desperate and dangerous. A number of skilled lifeguards have died attempting to save drowning victims. I know a valley with a spring fed stream running through it and populated with stands of big hardwoods and evergreens where the air is like champagne and breathing is a sensual experience. It is a sacred grove where Artemis dwells. The feminine, like breath, cannot be taken for granted. Robert Johnson in <u>Lying with the Heavenly Woman</u>, writes,

> Few men understand how important femininity is their lives, both inner and outer. Almost all of a man's sense of value, worth, safety, joy, contentment, belongingness, and happiness derive from his inner feminine nature. If God created male and female and gave them equal power (I like to translate the critical word rib as "side" or "half" in the Genesis story of the creation of Eve), the delicate and subtle half that is the province of femininity is as powerful as the masculine province.

Further on Johnson writes, "He (Jung) chose the term anima because it is her chief characteristic that she animates and gives life. ...femininity is the color and delight and animation of a man's life. Without femininity a man is poverty- stricken and without life. She is life."

A few years ago, I was caretaker on a twenty-acre estate. Rolling lawns shaded with huge trees, lovely flowerbeds, and two great dogs. The property backed on to a deep forest. But none of this beauty touched its owner. He would not let it in. It was just a possession for him and it gave him no joy. Just as he would not give himself to his lovely and loving wife.

He betrayed her with another woman. One look at his face and you knew he was an unhappy man. He was mired down in the hyper masculine, denying the feminine and diminishing his life.

Why do we men do this? Because the guy code will not have it. It is not the right stuff. Even worse, it smacks of faggotry. Our fear of homosexuality and of being effeminate keeps us from experiencing our feminine, from cultivating and caring for our anima, and so we soldier on, being "real men." If we would meet the our needs for our feminine, that emptiness will not be down there in the basement of our unconscious gathering dark force to be projected with compulsive need onto some beautiful woman whom we have made into a goddess. We, then, could come to a woman with love

A friend of mine has a wondrously beautiful daughter of eighteen, the most beautiful woman I have ever seen in my life. She has a face and body like a cathedral, but I, we men, must not desire her. We must look upon her as we do upon a beautiful flower or the woods and meadows in the valley here with the morning mist still hanging over the hollow down to the lake.

A beautiful woman brings us men close to sacred wonder or madness. We must choose. Some part of us would like to be Zeus surprising a beautiful young nymph bathing in some Aegean grotto and taking her. The code leaves us starved for beauty so that when we stand before the beauty of a woman we want to possess her rather than contemplating and rejoicing in her beauty, but the code does not know how to do this. The Feminine carries the beauty of life, the world and the awesome experience of being, itself. This is why so much art has been dedicated to the female nude.

Bernadine Jacot and Lian Hudson in their book, <u>The way Men Think</u>, state that Bonnard, the fine impressionist artist, would study the female body, "releasing from it its hidden store of light," that "hidden store of light' is the radiance of the feminine and that is why men have a problem with beauty as its energy resonates deep within their psyches.. A man has the problem of how to stand before "that hidden store of light" in women and to relate to the beauty which the feminine carries and, ultimately, to carry it within himself, within in his own Anima. On the deepest level, the masculine seeks communion and unity with beauty and the feminine, but many men do not know how to go about this so they resort to loutish and aggressive responses. A beautiful young woman told me of a car full of young men driving by her one evening and one of them hanging out the window yelling to her, "Hey, can I borrow your tits for a while?" He just could not handle the blaze of her beauty. He probably spoke for the whole carload of them. When I was an adolescent, a strip tease dancer (that's what they were called then) was shot in the breast with a BB gun. Very likely, a young man who felt that he, too, was outcast from the feast of life and so had gotten himself into a hostile state of mind with regard to women. Interesting that he shot her in the breast.

The feminine is the joyous connection with all that is. Our starved psyches want to possess them rather than to look upon them with joy and wonder like the flowers and leaves floating in my bowl. So our contemplation degenerates into lust. This is the problem of beauty, which the male psyche must resolve if it is ever to know serenity and the ability to relate to women in a loving manner. The starved male psyche sees beautiful women as denying them the congress with the feminine, which their soul craves. This is the beginning of their hostility and obsession with women. A number of times, I have sat at a table with a man as a beautiful young woman walked by as he said, "Look at that bitch." Where is that coming from?

Ruth Barnhouse's phrase, "the transition from male childhood to real manhood" is key. Real manhood, complete and full male identity, requires melding and interplay between his masculine and feminine components. Unfortunately, no formula or pat answer for doing this is available. It is a creative process. A man could start by learning something of the feminine and how to incorporate it onto himself. Incorporating the feminine is not the same as becoming feminine. He could start by throwing out that locker room mentality that maintains that the feminine is for wimps.

Ironically, the sensual experience, which every male, even locker room types, seeks, is the realm of the feminine. Sensual life is what the carefully prepared meals, the beautiful gardens and the arranged rooms are all about. One of the criticisms of modern life is that we are too preoccupied with sex and the sensual. In <u>The Soul of Sex</u>, Thomas Moore writes:

> We are obviously a sex-obsessed society. Why make it worse? In response, I call upon Freud...'we display outrageously and obsessively that which we do not fully possess or have deeply at our disposal.' If we are displaying sex with unseemly exaggeration and preoccupation, then we have not the heart of sex and not made it a fully integrated part of individual and social life.
>
> Given our obsession with sex, we need to get more of it, not in quantity but in quality. It's like a person addicted to junk food. He eats as much as he can because there is nothing there. If he were to eat real food   unprocessed, close to its earth origins, wonderfully prepared,   he might leave the addiction behind. We need more sex, not less, but we need sex with soul.

Moore's subtitle, "Cultivating Life as an Act of Love," is what the book is all about, which includes sex with soul and sensual, sexual life. All of this is the realm of the feminine. The body is in the realm of the feminine as is the whole of creation. A man who is stunted in the feminine and starved in these needs of the soul will be vulnerable to an illusion, a projection whereupon a certain woman will appear to have all of this for him. She will appear to be the only source and he will be desperate to have her. This is Jung's anima projection. The Soul of Sex is an extraordinary book; perhaps the first source a man might consult to cultivate his feminine. Changing one's metaphysics is not easy. It requires humility, admitting that we have been going in the wrong direction and seeking the wrong things. We have worked hard and long to become proficient in these wrong things. To change all that requires a major effort in an unknown direction. But not to change is an even greater risk.

Stephen Daedelus in James Joyce's autobiographical novel, A Portrait of the Artist as a Young Man, has got it right. Stephen is wrestling with his Irish patriarchal heritage and culture and its denial of beauty, wonder and sensual pleasure. Then he sees a young woman wading off the beach and he has an Epiphany, a moment of illuminated consciousness.

> He was alone. He was unheeded, happy and near to the wild heart of life. He was alone and young and wilful wildhearted, alone amid a waste of wild air and brackish waters and the seaharvest of shells and tangle and veiled grey sunlight and gayclad lightclad figures, of children and girls and voices childish and girlish in the air.
>
> A girl stood before him in midstream, alone and still, gazing out to sea. She seemed like one whom magic had changed into the likeness of a strange and beautiful seabird. Her long, slender, bare legs were delicate as a crane's and pure

save where an emerald trail of seaweed had fastened itself as a sign upon the flesh. Her thighs, fuller and softhued as ivory, were bared almost to the hips where the white fringes of her drawers were like the featherings of soft white down. Her slateblue skirts were kilted boldly about her waist and dovetailed behind her. Her bosom was as a bird's soft and slight, slight and soft as the breast of some dark plumaged dove. But her long fair hair was girlish: and girlish and touched with the wonder of mortal beauty, her face.

She was alone and still, gazing out to sea: and when she felt his presence and the worship of his eyes her eyes turned to him in quiet sufferance of his gaze, without shame or wantonness. Long, long she suffered his gaze and then quietly withdrew her eyes from his and bent them toward the stream, gently stirring the water with her foot hither and thither...and a faint flame trembled on her cheek.

Heavenly God! cried Stephen's soul, in an outburst of profane joy.

He turned away from her suddenly and set off across the strand. His cheeks were aflame: his body was aglow; limbs were trembling. On and on and on he strode, far out over the sands, singing wildly to the sea, crying to greet the advent of the life that had cried out to him.

Her image had passed into his soul forever and no word had broken the holy silence of his ecstasy; her eyes had called to him and his soul had leaped at the call. To live, to err, to fall, to triumph, to recreate life out of life! A wild angel had appeared to him... an envoy from the fair courts of life, to throw open before him in an instant of ecstasy the gates of all the ways of error and glory.

He felt...the earth beneath him, the earth that had borne him, had taken him to her breast.

He closed his eyes in the languor of sleep. His eyelids trembled...as if they felt the strange light of some new world.

Stephen has experienced something far beyond sexual desire as his soul cries out, "Heavenly God." He has let himself be touched by the Eternal Feminine, which reached out to him in the form of the girl on the beach. Her image, that touch has given him a heightened sense of being and unity with the holy splendour and beauty of life and he has embraced life in its totality. He knows now that life holds far more than what his patriarchal Irish culture allows. His soul has been seared and his eyes pealed. Stephen does not approach the young woman. Intuitively, he knows that she is the agency for this transcendental experience..., "an envoy from the fair courts of life," whose "image had passed into his soul forever." She is daughter of the Divine Feminine whose "eyes had called to him and his soul had leaped at the call."

Portrait of the Artist concludes as Stephen, his soul awakened, goes forth, his mother's prayer within him,

> ...that I may learn in my own life and away from home and friends, what the heart is and what it feels. Amen. So be it. Welcome, O life! I go to encounter for the millionth time the reality of experience and to forge in the smithy of my soul the uncreated consciousness of my race.

Stephen has done it right. His Epiphany has been an interior experience. He has taken it into himself. He does not pursue the girl. He does not seek to possess her. He understands that she represents the beauty and joy of life that he is to pursue and take onto himself. She is the agency of his inner experience, his awakening to the task before him, which is the task of every man, "to learn what the heart is and what it feels." This is his quest, our quest, for the feminine. Stephen goes to "encounter...the reality of experience." As he cries out, "Welcome, O life!" he sees he is to embrace life in its totality and "forge" this new consciousness "in the smithy of his soul." The realm of the feminine has opened up before Stephen and he totally accepts the challenge. This wondrous account of Stephen's expanded consciousness is why Portrait is one of the great modern novels.

Contrast Stephen's response to the girl on the beach with that of William Randolph Hurst when he saw the nineteen-year-old Marion Stephens in a Broadway chorus line and had a similar vision. She was his "wild angel," "his envoy from the fair courts of life." Hurst dazzled her with gifts, flowers, expensive restaurants, Rolls Royce's, and so on. He whisked her off to his mega million dollar estate, San Simion, on the California coast, and installed her there as his mistress. He literally purchased her off that Broadway stage. He sought to possess her, to have her, which was destructive to the both of them. He was extremely jealous of her and would not permit her to have a life of her own. She became an alcoholic. She was the prisoner of San Simion. He desperately tried to create a career for her in movies. It was a classic goddess trip and so it was a disaster for them both.

The power of beauty is not an easy thing for a man to handle. In The Brothers Karamazov, Dostoyevsky has Alyosha saying to Ivan as they stand before the portrait of the beautiful Grushenka, "Beauty is the battleground where God and the Devil fight for the heart of man."

Every man must wrestle with the problem of beauty. It is a battleground where many men fail. Our culture, largely shaped by the patriarchal mind, has taken us far from unity, connection, beauty and the feminine, nevertheless, the memory of it, as we had it with our mothers, is still imprinted on our deepest early memories. All this is associated with the memory of our mother's face, the contours and softness of her body and breasts. Beauty, particularly that of a beautiful young woman, conjures all that up from deep within us. All this old yearning and need imprinted on us even before we were born, we bring into our relationships and even to a brief encounter with a woman. It is not easy to keep the beauty of woman in perspective. My friend's beautiful daughter is "an envoy from the fair courts of life." She, too, is a daughter of the Divine Feminine. The feminine is the joyous connection with all that is. Harville Hendrix in <u>Keeping the Love You Find</u>, has a section entitled, "The Cosmic Journey: Yearning for Connection", where he writes:

> ...those moments of grandeur and deep joy we occasionally have with our child or camping under a star filled summer sky or a time of love with our companion. In these moments, we have escaped the boundaries and limits, which we have accrued from everyday life and are in touch our real selves and the full depths of our being.... Mysterious and elusive as such moments are, they tell us something important about who we are as human beings, and about the parts of us that are hidden behind the veil of our every day reality, all of which has profound impact on our relationships.
>
> The source of our difficulties in relationships does not originate with our partner. What happened to us, as children cannot explain the inchoate, tidal emotions of falling in love or the great pain we feel at its loss. We have to look elsewhere for an explanation of the foetal experience. The foetus has no experience of itself, no awareness of a separation from its mother, no past, no future. There is only now, oneness and unity on an oceanic scale.

Then Hendrix asks, "But isn't this notion of our timeless connection to everything a bit far fetched? Aren't we crossing over into mumbo jumbo territory here?" He is voicing the objections of the patriarchal mind, and then he answers them with, "I don't think so."

The macho guys immediately write off any such feelings and thoughts of cosmic unity as sheer rubbish and loss of contact with reality, which for them is the bottom line of their next quarterly report. This sense of the deep unity of all things is the realm of the feminine. The patriarchal mind will have none of it because it poses too great a threat to its convictions of how things are. The feminine is too great a threat to patriarchal power and control and just too great a challenge to the metaphysics they live by.

But a number of great thinkers have spoken of this unity. William James in <u>The Varieties of Religious Experience: A Study in Human Nature,</u>

> We, with our lives, are like islands in the sea, like the trees in the forest. The maple and the pine may whisper to each other with their leaves...But the trees also commingle their roots in the darkest underground, and the islands also hang together through the ocean's bottom. Just so there is a continuum of cosmic consciousness, against which our individuality builds but accidental fences...Our normal consciousness is circumscribed for adaptation to external environment, but the fence is weak in spots, and fitful influences from beyond leak in, showing the otherwise unverifiable human connection.

This metaphysical and mysterious connection is the realm of the feminine. The academic language of James fails to communicate the sheer power and wonder of this connection and unity. It is there and we men have been ignoring it for a long time to our detriment and peril. Our culture and Male Code in no way prepares us to seek this unity and connection.

All this old yearning, imprinted on us even before we were born, we bring into our lives and our relationships. Joseph Campbell said, "It as always been said that human beings have been searching for the meaning of life, but what we are really searching for is the feeling of aliveness. It is not meaning, that we seek, but unity and connection." The desire to be fully alive and connected with the life force is a powerful, archetypal drive. If we do not feel that, we have to do something, buy something, eat too much, gamble, take drugs, drink, get laid, turn up the music. An ecstasy user said when she took the drug, she felt, "connected to everyone else." Our psyches are driven to fill the gap and to pursue "the unity and the connection" of which Campbell, James and Hendrix speak.

When we men reject the feminine, we reject this vital consciousness and so we live a partial life, a part of us is then unlived. The unlived life has consequences. Recall Jung speaking of "the revenge of the unlived life." The psyche becomes starved for that which it does not have and must have. At that point a beautiful woman becomes the symbol in our psyche for everything, which has eluded us in this life. We must have her. We become prime candidates for obsession.

Susan Forward and Craig Buck's Obsessive Love is a brilliant book. Chapter Eight is entitled: "Connection Compulsion: The Root of Obsessive Love." A section of which is entitled, "The Blissful Connection", another section is, "When Separation Gets Derailed."

> If the separation process can be so easily disturbed in healthy families, imagine what happens if our parents frighten us, hurt us, abuse us, or neglect us on a regular basis. Such parents sabotage our separation by damaging the self-confidence, and the confidence in others, that we need on the path to independence. If we grow up in an unhealthy family in an atmosphere where our needs for respect, love, approval, and protection are generally ignored or trampled, the disconnection process is more than interrupted, it is almost certainly derailed.

This derailment sets up what Forward and Buck call, "The Connection Compulsion." This is a sexual relationship which appears to be a reconnection and it becomes charged with all that need which has been buried deep down in the unconscious all these years and becoming more and more urgent with time. All that goes into a man's Goddess Projection, his Anima Projection which is often ready to go, like the guy in a New York Times article on dating, who said on a first date, "I've missed you," or it can produce an intense almost dream like state. Recall Constable Hotte saying, "It was like I was in the dark." This emotional charge can be strong enough to compel obsessive and even violent behavior as in the case of Hotte and O.J. Simpson. But a beautiful woman is not the only illusion on which the starved male psyche can fixate. The next two chapters, "Macho Sport, Macho Politics" and "Selfhood, the Sacred Work," will further explore the consequences of the pursuit of the false self and the macho denial of the feminine. They are all short circuits to obsession and disaster of one sort or another.

CHAPTER SEVEN

Macho Sport, Macho Politics

Varda Burstyn's <u>The Rites of Men: Manhood, Politics, and the Culture of Sport is</u> brilliant on the depth and power of the macho culture and mentality, She calls the macho and patriarchal model of masculinity "hypermasculinity," and defines it as, "...the belief that manhood lies in the exercise of force to dominate others... (It is) the prevalent ideology of manhood in contemporary male society."

This chapter is a critique of this ideology and in no way do I intend to deny the fine constructive role sports can play in affirming both masculine and feminine identity. The concentration and confidence required to play my best have been good for me. Sports have played a valuable part in my life and that of many of my friends. This chapter is about what the hypermasculine does with sport.

Burstyn sees sports as a major arena where the macho credo is played out. Sports occupy a huge place in the male collective psyche, culture and mythology. When the U.S. space probe, Sojourner, landed on Mars in July 1997 sending back photographs of the surface, the NASA official compared this to "winning the Super bowl, the World Cup and the World Series." He could find nothing greater than the winning of these sporting events to describe the magnitude of this momentous scientific and historical achievement.

The most recognizable faces in the world are frequently

athletic superstars like Tiger Woods, Michael Jordan, Wayne Gretsky and so on. Reliable estimates place the electronic attendance of the 1996 Atlanta Olympics at between two and three billion people close to half the population of the planet. Sport results and scores are reported right along with national and world events on our daily newscasts. Sports are huge in our culture and in the collective male mind. The place given to sports is accepted as totally natural and not given a second thought.

Burstyn speaks of "sport as secular sacrament." She quotes sports psychologist Saul Miller at a Denver Bronco's football game "while 75,000 fans roared and the team romped under its 40 foot Bronco mascot." Miller was on the field and looked up at this huge horse up there painted orange. "I swear it looked like the great god Ba'al or something. It was their tribe, and they chanted and sang." ESPN advertised its football broadcasts with this copy spoken over an image of a football player kneeling, head bowed, in front of a huge filled stadium, "Join our congregation this Sunday for an inspirational experience."

When I was preparing for the Catholic priesthood, we wore a cassock and Roman collar. I was asked to lead a prayer before a local football game in Houston, Texas. I sensed that this sacramentalizing of this football game was bizarre, and I declined. Victory for the home team becomes, at times, a pseudo transcendent experience for the fans. Baker, in <u>Sports in the Western World,</u> wrote, "Marching bands, majorettes and cheerleaders took the field as supporting casts for the athletes. College football in the Roaring Twenties became an autumn ritual. Harper's observed, "It is at present a religion, sometimes it seems to be almost our national religion."

Billions of dollars have been put into domed stadiums,

which have become the cathedrals of macho culture. U.S. coffin makers manufacture caskets in the colors of Alabama, Auburn, Georgia and Tennessee. The promotional copy reads, "For that final touchdown." Can these people be serious? Are they listening to themselves? This is material for the Comedy Channel.

Sport has achieved mythic proportions in our society. Just because we don't believe in Zeus anymore doesn't mean we don't have myths. Myth is like a dream of the collective psyche as it attempts to resolve the great questions and mysteries of life. Myths proceed out of that wrestling with these matters. They are a symbolic representation. The rites of sport are a symbolic representation of the questions of manhood, sexuality and male identity. The struggle to win has become the test of manhood and the laurel wreath of victory is the public affirmation of the excellence of one's manhood and person. Robert Brannon has defined the macho code of manhood as:

1.   No sissy stuff: Men can never do anything that even remotely suggests femininity. Manhood is a relentless repudiation of the feminine.

2.   Be a big wheel: manhood is measured by power, wealth and success. Who ever has the most toys when he dies wins.

3   Be a sturdy oak: manhood depends on emotional reserve. Dependability in a crisis requires that men not reveal their feelings.

4.   Give 'em hell: exude an aura of manly daring and aggression. Go for it. Take risks.

Sport has achieved a mythic place in the male psyche because it plays out all four aspects of the credo. Sport is a major subset of the macho culture. Sport, where winning, that is dominating and defeating the opponent, is everything. Power and domination is the proof and stamp of manhood. Playing the game for its own sake has receded very far into the background.

Athletic excellence and winning is so important to some athletes that any risk is justified. Many contact sport athletes have permanent injuries especially to knees, back and, even worse, brain damage. But contact sports are the ultimate test and the highest rung on the macho juggernaut. Boxers say, "You play baseball, basketball and football. You don't play boxing." This is not all together true. On the competitive level, these games are not play. They are ritualized warfare. Then there is Rodeo; those guys really bang themselves up for the Code. Their motto is, "Basketball, Baseball, Football, Rodeo-Bring your own balls."

No risk is too great in the quest for macho manhood: not the damage to health, longevity, reputation, even the risk of sexual impotency posed by the use of steroids and other banned substances. The widespread use of these substances demonstrates how prevalent and deeply ingrained this mentality is with many men. Their use has seriously undermined the integrity of professional, amateur and even Olympic sport.

Burstyn quotes Michael Bamberger and Don Yeager's Sports Illustrated article, "Over the Edge":

> Even casual fans notice that NBA players sport biceps that a Kevin McHale ...never dreamed of; that Ivy League colleges field football teams with linemen bigger than All Pro linemen were a few years ago; and that it is no longer remarkable for veteran big league baseball players to show up at spring training having put on 20 pounds of solid muscle since the end of the previous season... Steroid use and other,

more exotic substances, such as human growth hormone has spread to almost every sport, from major league baseball to college basketball to high school football. It is the dirty and universal secret of sports, amateur and pro...

Bob Goldman's famous "two scenarios" survey given to 198 Olympic class athletes says a great deal as well:

Scenario I: You are offered a banned performance enhancing substance, with two guarantees. 1. You will not be caught. 2. You will win. Would you take the substance? One hundred ninety five said yes.

Scenario II: You are offered a banned performance enhancing substance that comes with two guarantees. 1. You will not be caught. 2. You will win every competition you enter for the next five years and then you will die from the side effects of the substance. Would you take it? More than half of the men said yes.

This survey is conducted every two years with close results every time. With these athletes, winning is of greater value than longevity. The article quotes Dutch sport physician, Michael Karstan, "If you are especially gifted, you may win once. But from my experience, you can't continue to win without drugs. The field is just too filled with drug users."

The article concludes that despite the scandals, the testing and the determination of Olympic sport, the use of these banned drugs is even more widespread than it was in the late 1980's. All of this is sad testimony to the self-destructive priority given to winning and the macho image of manhood. The good Arnold Schwartzenager has spoken on winning "You do everything you can to win, whatever it takes." He understands these things, and now he is Governor of California elected on little more than his macho image.

But there is only so much room on the playing field, so for those without the prowess to play the sport there is total identification with a team. The force of this identification is shown in the rabid exploits of British 'soccer hooligans' in the 80's conducting gang warfare, rioting and even killing in various European capitals to the degree that many of these fans are banned in a number of countries. The routine violence and mayhem associated with these matches required mounted police and even army contingents. The Heyschel Stadium massacre was the most famous of these incidents, but there were hundreds of others. There were instances where the stadiums gave way under the stress of the rioting and hundreds of people were killed and thousands more injured.

This sort of rabid identification is not limited to the Brit football fan. When the Detroit Pistons won the 1990 NBA championship, seven people were killed in the riots that followed. In June 1993, four people were killed in Chicago when the Chicago Bulls won the championship. Chicago won again in 1997, and three people were killed. These are serious symptoms of a collective near insanity that cannot be ignored. They illustrate how close sports, winning and violence reside in the psyches of many men because sports define manhood as the forceful domination of others. The identification with a team serves only as a focal point for the violence. Violence is the thing and is the common denominator between victory on the court and the mayhem afterward. It is all about violence as the stuff of manhood.

Harper's, May 2003, issue, has this chilling description of a video game, Hooligans Over Europe, recently released by the Dutch company Darxabre coming out in time for the World Cup that summer. This is from their promotional website:

PRACTICE MAKES PERFECT

The Game: The object is to become the most notorious group of hooligans in Europe. You must kill, maim, and destroy the opposing Hooligan teams. You must muster and control your faithful troops by administering drugs, alcohol, and, of course a good dose of violence every now and then. Not only are good strategic skills required, but also a good political mindset and managing capabilities to keep your troops happy and violent. Whoever is victorious and catches the public's attention in the media will end up the most notorious Hooligans in Europe and the world – a title that every Hooligan with his heart in the right place lives to fight for!

Game – play: It is up to you to find out how to get the most out of them. You can do a lot with your units: get them into a fight, make them loot or destroy buildings, get them drunk, give them dope, buy weapons for them, etc.

The units will feel more comfortable when they are in a group. Single units or small groups are likely to get scared if they face a threatening situation. When fear is high, they will run away when they are attacked, however, if you give them an order they will do what they are told. When a unit receives damage, it will become angry. Units also tend to get angry when they have had a lot of beer. When units are angry, they will want to fight and attack other units they see, unless you give them another order. Drunk units are difficult to control and sometimes they can't stop from falling over. So what is the use of drunk units? If units are drunk they are less likely to get scared and more likely to get angry.

Giving units dope can give you a great advantage over your opponents. They are less vulnerable and their stamina stays at top level. Watch out, though, your units can die from taking too much of the stuff. When you are playing, you will see little icons over the heads of the units. We call them "emoticons." They indicate the dominant state of the unit. So you can see if a unit is drunk or angry or doped up or madly in love.

At every level, you will start out with one leader and a couple of units. You can go to pubs to get more men, if you need them. Of course, they will need a little convincing, and it will cost you more than a couple fivers. To keep your cash flow going, you can loot shops. Obviously the police are not too happy about this and will try to punish you when they find out. You will also need money to buy weapons or drugs. It is possible to steal these by looting the shop, but sometimes the price is high! The dope house sells some nice stuff to "stimulate" your units. In the dreadful event that one of your units gets hurt, you can send him to a house of pleasure. Inside he can get a nice healing "massage" and will be in good shape in no time!

It is up to you to find a suitable strategy to complete the levels. Remember, most stuff you do is highly illegal, and the police will have both eyes open. Most of the time it is not very wise to start messing around with the police. They take every excuse to beat the crap out of you or throw you in jail!

Violent video games like Grand Theft Auto, where points are given for killing a policeman, have sales in the billions. Another game awards points for decapitating a victim and having sex with a prostitute, then killing her.

The culture of contact sports and of macho masculinity is close to a school for rape. Former football player Allen Sack, quoted by Varda Burstyn in her Ideas, CBC radio program, October, 1986, said:

I played football from the time I was in seventh grade until I graduated from college ... I think we ...almost learn rape from our young male athletic experiences. In other words, we learn that when a woman in the back seat of a car is saying no, no, no, I don't want to do this, we learn on the contrary, to push it farther. ... And I think often times athletic behaviour, even more than ordinary behavior, socializes young males not to understand those kind of boundaries ... We dominate opponents, we dominate other athletes, we dominate our friends on the athletic field, and of course, we dominate women.

A number of feminists have referred to "the rape culture" and a number of studies bear them out. Rick Hoffman writing in the Philadelphia Daily News, "Rape and the College Athlete," found that a college athlete was reported for sexual assault once every eighteen days on average between 1983 and 1986. "Football and Basketball players representing NCAA schools were reported to police for sexual assault approximately 38 percent more often than the average male on a college campus." Michael Messner noted, "...when verbal sparring and bragging about sexual conquests led to actual behavior, peer group values encouraged these young men to treat females as objects of conquest." Robin Warshaw in I Never Called it Rape, states that athletic teams are breeding grounds for rape, "There is a masculine peer group dynamic, which affirms that the domination and control of women is a mark of manhood and the entitlement of men. This dynamic creates the rape culture."

The macho culture has forged powerful beliefs in physical force and the elite entitlement of men. It is part of the code. Currently, the media is mesmerized by the trial of Kobe Brant, one time poster boy for Mr. Clean of the NBA, now accused of rape, his world is crashing down around him as million dollar endorsements are flying out the window, and his reputation is in tatters. He listened to the boys in the locker room who told him, "We are entitled to any woman we want. We are NBA jocks." If it was, like he says, consensual sex, then what he did was betray his loving wife and mother of his child for a little extra curricular sex. He was acquitted, but, still, it was a nasty business. He learned a hard lesson that listening to the boys in the locker room is a big mistake. Very sad, he looks like he has been deep into the macho sport scene from an early age. He looks like he wishes he hadn't done it, whatever it was. The macho fan frequently identifies with an individual player. Kolby's rape accuser and judge in the hearing received death threats from outraged fans. The violence spills over from the sports stadium into the streets and into the home. Alisa DelTufo, the founder of Sanctuary for Families, a shelter for abused women and children in New York City said,

> The pursuit of dominance lies at the heart of all athletic contests, and it happens to be the animating force behind men who batter their women. Men who need to be in control...in order to feel O.K. about themselves often have a problem with domestic violence.

Nack and Munson quoted Charles Barkley after the Philadelphia 79ers scarcely defeated the New Jersey Nets on Nov. 3, 1990, "This is a game that, if you lose you go home and beat your wife and kids." Joe Paterno, a Penn State football coach, after a team loss on Sept. 8, 1990 said, "I'm going home to beat my wife."

Failing to beat their opponents, at least they can beat their families. With many athletes, the violence in their athletics validates their sexual violence. These writers conclude, "An athlete cherishes nothing more that control over an opponent, and nothing lifts him higher than the sense that he has attained that control." The macho athletic culture promotes that control in every aspect of a man's life. These men, who desperately need to be in control, have the least control where they need it the most: namely inside their own heads, inside their own psyches. Because they have denied fundamental laws and requirements of the psyche, they are out of control.

Because they lack an inner feminine component to their psyche, they must dominate women in an unconscious attempt to take possession of her femininity and thus complete themselves. Violence becomes an affirmation of identity, an experience of a man's being alive. Writer Bill Buford joined one of the English football clubs in the 1980's to observe and document first hand the dynamics of this violence. In his book, <u>Among the Thugs</u>, he writes, "Violence is one of the most intensely lived experiences and for those capable of giving themselves over to it, is one of the most intense pleasures." Buford sees the lives of these fans as permeated with a "desperate bleakness" and "deadened" perhaps to the point of needing "violence to wake up... The lad culture of British football pricks itself so it has feeling, burns its flesh so it has smell."

Love is a feminine quality. Violence becomes a way of denying love and renouncing the feminine. That renunciation is one of the tenets of hypermasculine male identity. Ted Crosset, professor of Sports Management at the University of Massachusetts, writes, "Part of the male athlete's subworld is not to be a woman. Women are degraded. You don't want to be skirt of the week. Women are not to be respected. Women are despised."

The military has bought this definition of manhood big time. Only real men are any good at soldiering. Drill sergeants attempt to shame male recruits into manhood as they yell at them, "Ladies, attention." The novelist, Tim O'Brien, describes his basic training at Fort Lewis. He and a friend were sitting alone polishing their boots when their sergeant came up and screamed at them, "A couple of college pussies, out behind the barracks hiding from everyone and making love, huh? You afraid to be in the war, a goddamn pussie, a goddam lezzie?" A drill sergeant at Fort Jackson, SC, screamed at recruit struggling with push-ups, "So, are we having menstrual cramps this morning?"

Female recruits got the same treatment, "You wuss, you baby, you goddam female" Fort Jackson, 1991. Their femininity was likewise despised. They were supposed to be men as in this hyped up model of masculinity. A model where hard is masculine and soft is not. Violence and anger are the acceptable feelings.

The psyche is driven to possess an identity, because these men have failed to achieve an authentic identity they take on to this hyped up model. They have to have something, but this stunted vicarious identity has consequences. John Gilligan writes, "Statistically, most lethal violence is committed by men against other men... Violence is primarily men's work; it is carried out more frequently against men and it is about the maintenance of "manhood."

There it is: violence as "the maintenance of manhood." Schwartzenager, in the "Terminator" movies, is an android machine programmed to kill a certain woman, in order to change the history of the future. The great success of the Terminator movies, in the hundreds of millions, with largely male audiences, says a great deal.

William Broyles in an Esquire, November 1984, article about his Vietnam experiences, "Why men Love War" writes: "war is, for men, at some terrible level, the closest thing to what childbirth is for women: the initiation into the power of life and death."

A feeling expressed by NFL lineman Marvin, who when asked how he could endure such punishment for so many years, replied:

> You know, a lot of people look at a lineman and they say, 'Oh, man, you gotta be some kind of animal to get down there and beat on each other like that.' But it's just like a woman

> giving birth ...I think it's something that's an act of God, that's
> unreal. But she hasn't done nothing she wasn't built for...Now
> here I am, 260, 270 pounds, and that's my position... That's
> what I'm built for. Just like a truck carrying a big Caterpillar:
> you see the strain, but that's what it's built for.

This man sees himself created for the violence of NFL line. This is what men do.

The issue of gun control, totally loaded both emotionally and politically, is not really about guns or protection or sport; it is about macho manhood and what the cold-machined steel and latent violence of their weapons represents deep in their psyches. The National Rifle Association raises hundreds of millions of dollars to rabidly lobby and campaign against even the mildest and most reasonable measures of gun control because the issue taps into the vicarious manhood of these men. Very few politicians have the courage and integrity to take on the NRA over this. It is generally considered political suicide and it often has been. The actor, Charlton Heston, president of the NRA frequently lectures to these people, rallying them with the cry as holds his Winchester lever action over his head with both hands, "They will have to take it from these cold, dead hands." In other words, "Nobody messes with our virility."

Broyles writes,

> War is a brutal, deadly game, but War may be the only
> way in which most men touch the mythic domains in our
> soul...If you come back you bring with you the knowledge that
> you have explored regions of your soul that in most men will
> always remain uncharted... A game, the best there is...

"A game, the best there is..." Joseph Campbell wrote, "We seek not the meaning of life, but the experience of being alive." For these men, whose feelings have been denied and frozen in their quest for macho manhood, and the adrenalin rush brought on by their brush with violence and danger is their only way of experiencing any kind of heightened awareness, any kind of feeling life. For these men, it is "the best there is." The adrenalin rush is the only acceptable feeling to the macho paradigm of masculinity. Broyles goes on to say, "The love of war stems from the union, deep in the core of our being, between sex and destruction, beauty and horror love and death.... War is, in short, a turn on."

The metaphysics of macho manhood spills over into the male dominated world of politics and government. The historian, Geoffrey Smith, in <u>Diplomatic History</u>, called Lyndon B. Johnson and Richard Nixon "the two toughest hombres of them all." Further, he writes,

> Johnson's policies in Vietnam were peppered with sexual references, as the Texan defended his masculinity against adversaries at home and in Southeast Asia. After an American bombing campaign in 1965, he boasted, 'I didn't just screw Ho Chi Minh, I cut his pecker off.' Johnson also had little use for the 'nervous nellies,' persons who questioned his policies, and therefore lacked the necessary sexual equipment. Of one in-house dove, Johnson explained, 'Hell, he has to squat to piss.'
>
> Nixon was an even harsher patriarch. His administration nurtured a cult of toughness, underscoring the need to punish dissenters." During Nixon's administration, football imagery had become the root metaphor. The secret service requires a code name for the president. Nixon chose "Quarterback." He named an Air Force B-52 operation in Vietnam, "Linebacker." He would regularly telephone the coach of the Washington Redskins to discuss strategy before big games. Nixon blamed the U.S. defeat in Vietnam on the "gutless" and "feminine" attitudes prevalent in the country as well as "emotion, weakness, inaction, negotiation and compromise", all negative features of the feminine in his mind. Nixon's "Peace With Honor" was a euphemism for terms with macho pride intact.

Even John F. Kennedy whose administration has been called by many, "the best and the brightest," was dominated by the requirement to be tough. Barbara Tuchman writing in The <u>March of Folly: from Troy to Vietnam,</u> "The new men in government, whether Rhoades Scholars, academics from Harvard and Brookings or recruits from Wall Street, politics and the Law, were expected to be realistic, sophisticated, pragmatic, tough. Toughness was the tone, and...Kennedy's group adapted it, as the court around a monarch or a working group around a dominate chief."

Tuchman quotes Robert McNamara: "We have the power to knock any society out of the 20th century." Adelaide Stevenson, one of the most capable men in modern American politics, was eliminated from the inner circle "because he was thoughtful (he) was seen as that unforgivable thing, 'soft'. It was this tough guy stance which led them all to make the first sizable U.S. intervention into Vietnam. It was the first step into the most catastrophic campaign in modern American history."

Then after Kennedy, Lyndon Johnson would not disengage from Vietnam because he was afraid that "Robert Kennedy would be out front telling everybody that I was a coward, an unmanly man, a man without a spine." Johnson thought he had to pursue this war in order to manifest his virility. That decision gutted his dream, "The Great Society," his domestic policy. It cost him his second term as president and his place in history as one of the great presidents.

Varda Burstyn, in her <u>Rites of Men</u>, writes of a conservatism which is little more than a mean spirited individualism and antisocial state policies are evident in North American neoconservative political culture in the 1980s, 1990s and right up to the present. The very rich are getting richer and the ordinary folks are getting poorer. The value given to power is reflected in our social and economic structure. Burstyn writes,

> In the late 1990's 358 individuals have a personal wealth equivalent to the combined wealth of the poorest 45 per cent of the world's population, when 50 of the world's 150 largest economies are corporations and weaponry and systems of war consume more than a trillion dollars a year...Power is condensed in enduring structures and economies that are based in staggering inequalities of power and privilege.

Now President Bush II is the front man and male cheerleader for this same mean spirited, very conservative, extremely wealthy political element that now has installed him in the West Wing. Now, while riding a crest of patriotism and national security following 9/11 and their war on terrorism, they are railroading through the conservative dream agenda: tax cuts for the very rich, stripping away the environmental protection which has been in the way of big corporate profits and pulling down the safety net for the disadvantaged and the dispossessed. The very rich are getting richer and the ordinary people are getting poorer. Bush's economic plan is: if we take care of the very rich, they will take care of us and America. This is the same kind of supply side economics that Bush Sr. called "voo doo economics" when he was running against Reagan for the Republican presidential nomination.

This brand of macho politics with its lust for power, control and the concentration of wealth is a threat to the delicate fabric of our society, our economics, our well-being, our whole world. These critical times cannot afford the politics of male conquest and garnering of power. The Bush agenda is the dream macho agenda of power, domination and concentration of wealth. In spite of his looting of the nation's wealth and economic well being with his cuts for the very wealthy and huge military spending, his polling numbers ran high for years, because his handlers learned to exploit the macho mentality of most of the electorate. Finally, now, May 2006, the spin on his image has worn thin and his approval numbers have dropped to below thirty percent.

In 1991, his father decided he was going to war with Iraq. Again Burstyn:

> Bush decided he was going out there to, in his own words, "kick some ass." (For some time Bush had been called "a wimp," and now it was time to put an end to that. - PMH) He needed public support so he turned to the NFL. The (1991 Super bowl) game between the Buffalo Bills and the New York Giants was ultimately staged as a was spectacle,...a rousing rendition of the national anthem by Whitney Houston and a rousing half time speech by President Bush...
>
> The Super bowl was collaboratively produced and cosponsored in truly Orwellian fashion by the NFL, corporate television and government. It delivered pure pro war propaganda to...750 million people... The entire five-hour broadcast was one massive infomercial for war, for warlike masculinity and its machines and institutions.

Curry Jansen and Sabo in their article, "The Sport/War Metaphor" observed,

> The press briefing room in the field closely resembled the set used by producers of television sport media for pre and post game analyses and interviews with coaches of professional football teams. The sport/war metaphors through military discourse and media coverage of the Gulf War were so blatant that both U.S. and Canadian networks ran commentary on the phenomenon. War reporting began to use the conventions of sports broadcasts... War became sport and vice versa.

The military has learned much since Vietnam where they alienated the media by stonewalling them. They know now that they must win them over and that sports macho is the way to do it. The First Gulf War didn't work so they had to do a second one, which is not working either. So now they had to pump it up. On May 12, 2003, they had Bush land on the Aircraft carrier, Abraham Lincoln, in a US Navy jet, tail hook and all, followed up with photo ops of our top gun president, in his flight suit, talking it up with his fellow pilots. The Abraham Lincoln was only twenty-four miles off San Diego, in sight of the shoreline. Knowledgeable journalists, particularly the British, could scarcely contain their laughter at this flagrant posturing. Elizabeth Bushmiller, writing in the New York Times, May 15, 2003, called it, "One of the most audacious moments of presidential theatre in American history."

But the grim reality is that this obvious manipulation, spin and public relations sells like free beer. His handlers are working the same mother lode as the very successful Brit laddie magazines, Maxim, Stuff and FHM, whose central themes are babes, beer, gear, sports and abs. Bush and Co. have discovered the magic of laddie politics.

Yesterday, July 3, 2003, President Bush, speaking of the more than two dozen "hostile" military deaths since the end of the war in Iraq, said, "...there are some who feel like the conditions are such that they can attack us there. My answer is: Bring 'em on." U.S. Representative Richard Gephardt criticized Bush for his "phoney, macho rhetoric" and his "shoot from the hip" one-liners. Senator Kerry responded, "The deteriorating situation in Iraq requires less swagger and more thoughtfulness and statesmanship." Bush's tough guy response to this exceedingly volatile situation is dangerous and it demonstrates how prevalent this hyper macho mentality is, even in government, affecting critical policy. Since Bush's tough talk, the casualties of U.S. troops have increased substantially. Now, June 2006, U.S. fatalities since the end of the war have exceeded 2500 and we are still counting. In Iraq, we are dealing with a massive clash of cultures and ideological fanatics. They are not going to be intimidated by George W. "Bring it on" Bush. A very different and intelligent approach is required. An approach these men do not understand in the least. Even mainstream media, like Newsweek, are beginning to think along these lines. The September 1, 2003 issue has an article, "Where Do We Go From Here?" with the headline, "It is time for America to recognize that the occupation of Iraq needs fixing. This has been a massive enterprise undertaken with little planning and extreme arrogance." Bush, Cheney and Co. are ruthless men who have no core except the macho code of power, control and domination, and that code projected into an extremely volatile region like the Middle East is a prescription for disaster.

A recent political cartoon, a bit of gallows humor, has a headshot of President Bush in front of the American flag. He is wearing dark glasses and an open leather jacket exposing an oiled manly chest. His mouth is slightly open, but not smiling. He is holding up a massive automatic pistol, could be a .44 magnum. The copy reads, "In the year of darkness, 2001, America devised the ultimate plan. He would reshape the future by ridding the world of an evil that felt nothing but hate. He was THE TURBANATOR."

It's a great send up of those Swartzenagger Terminator macho action vengeance flicks, but it is gallows humor because this stuff is dangerous, spilling over into our politics where it can do some real damage.

Thomas de Zengotita is talking about the same thing in his Harper's essay, April 2003, "The Romance of Empire,"

> You've noticed how, in those action vengeance flicks, there has to be this moment near the beginning when some very bad guys, led by this incredibly bad guy slaughter the partner or wife or even the kiddies, so that Seagal or Diesel can emerge fully justified, seared by a transcendent loss, by a grievance no judgment can encompass, commit mayhem for the rest of the movie, that being what you came to see in the first place? You've noticed that? You pay for the thrill of relentless carnage by enduring a few moments of sickening bathos... Seagal tossing a baseball with his soon to be rubbed out son, doom hanging over the scene, the lingering close-ups of that innocent face under Seagal's tender supervisory gaze, the awesome martial arts prowess tucked away for now. The Man at Home.

George W. Bush serves this emotional/ethical dynamic, and so do those who follow him. Their grievance is 9/11. They know who the bad guys are and they're going after them. It's pay back time. In George W.'s immortal words, "Bring em on." He is The Turbinator.

De Zengotita leads off that essay quoting Lieutenant General Jay Garner: "You ought to be beating your chest every morning. You ought to look in the mirror, suck in our bellies, and say, "Damn, we're Americans!" General Garner was George W.'s choice to restore order to post war Iraqi. He was fired a few months later. We never heard why. These people are defining America in these terms. Either you go along with it or you are no patriot. It is nasty stuff and it is dangerous.

Bob Hurbert writing in the New York Times, August 21, 2003, the day after the suicide bombing of the U.N. headquarters in Baghdad, quotes a high-ranking U.N. official,

This is dream for jihad, the resistance will only grow. The American occupation is now the focal point, drawing people from all over Islam into an eye-to-eye confrontation with the hated Americans." Now we are lodged in Iraq, in the midst of the most volatile region of the world, and the illusion of a quick victory followed by grateful Iraqis' welcoming us with open arms has vanished... the payoff of a policy spun from fantasies and lies.

A U.N. Aid told Hurbert, "The United States is the No. 1 enemy of the Moslem world, and right now it is sitting on the terrorist doorstep..." Jessica Stern writing in the New York Times, summed it up with, "America has taken a country that was not a terrorist threat and turned it into one."

Recently, Hunter S. Thompson had some penetrating commentary on the current political situation. Granted HST's authority may be open to some question considering his rather extraordinary life style, but, nevertheless, he did write <u>Fear and Loathing on the Campaign Trail '72</u>, a classic on American electoral politics, and Modern Classics publishes him. The man is not without credentials and the sheer power and insight of these observations might be considered.

"This nation is in the worst condition I can remember in my lifetime and our prospects for the immediate future even worse..."

"Iraqi is a tar baby."

"They have squandered the American dream."

Thompson quotes a Bob Dylan song,   "There is

something going on here, Mr. Jones and you don't even know what it is, do you?" Thompson speaks of "the downward spiral of dumbness in America." It is not going to be easy for macho America to admit that they bought and voted for, as Thompson puts it, "this goofy, child president we have on our hands now." "He is demonstrably a fool and a failure." But no one is going to look at that reality nor the reality of what Bush and Co. have been doing to this country as long as he lands on the flight deck of a carrier and jumps out in his flight suit. Bush's handlers understand these things totally. They understand the dumbing down of macho America and what can be done with it. Most people will dismiss Thompson's stuff as extreme raving, but a close look at what Bush and Co. have been doing will substantiate everything Thompson is saying. It is evident they have been cooking the input from the intelligence agencies to justify the invasion of Iraqi

. On domestic policy, Bob Hubert wrote in the July 29, 2003, New York Times,

> One of the things President Bush knows best is when to turn on the klieg lights and when to keep them off.   On Tuesday with no fanfare, he signed a bill increasing the federal debt limit by nearly a trillion dollars. You don't want a lot of coverage when you are mortgaging the future.
>
> But it was high fives all around as Mr. Bush signed the largest tax cut in history at a grand ceremony in the East Room of the White House. ...What the economy needs is a real stimulus that will create real jobs, not an irresponsible package of tax cuts that will inflate the portfolios of the very wealthy...
>
> We are closing schools and libraries in America, and withholding life saving drugs and medical treatment from the poor. The middle class is struggling ever harder to make ends meet, and reshaping its dreams of the future.
>
> In Washington they are celebrating.

Like HST says, Bush, Cheney and Co. "have squandered the American dream," and "Iraq is a tar baby." Our troops are being sniped at and killed daily in a near guerrilla war that is a nightmare with oil and water pipelines sabotaged and a society out of control. Anyone who has been paying attention these last few months could easily put together ten pages more to back up Hunter's conclusions. It is time to wake up. These are dangerous times, far too dangerous for the macho politics and jingoistic patriotism of these men. These are very dangerous men in a dangerous state of mind formed by the macho code.

CHAPTER EIGHT

Selfhood - the Sacred Work

When I was in the Seminary, I read Teilard de Chardin's The Divine Milieu. One passage resonated within me with its profound truth and reality.

> Thus every man must build - starting with the most natural territory of his own self - a work, an opus, into which something enters from all the elements of the earth. He makes his own soul through all his earthly days; and at the same time he collaborates in another work, in another opus, which infinitely transcends ... his individual achievement: the completing of the world ... Beneath our efforts to put spiritual form into our own lives, the world slowly accumulates...that which will make of it...the new earth.

Reading this passage of de Chardin, I felt in the presence of something holy, a fragment of sacred consciousness. What Rudolph Otto, in The Idea of the Holy, called the "misterium tremendum". The Vatican didn't know what to do with something this profound so they silenced de Chardin; he couldn't teach or publish.

To the typical macho, jockstrap, locker room male, Chardin is a voice coming from outer space. To these men, Chardin's vision of building a self is utter gibberish. They better understand Arnold Swartzenager, who, as he pulled up in one of the first civilian versions of the Hummer combat vehicle in Los Angeles, said, "Image is everything." This is why many of these men, will take steroids to build up their muscle mass in spite of the risk to their health, sexual potency and longevity. This image, this "cosmetic masculinity", to use Susan Faluti's apt term, is the very stuff of their selfhood.

To be, to have a self, is perhaps the greatest need and drive of any person, particularly a male. But a self-comprised of image and externals, has little substance to support itself. To have a self, to be actively engaged in creating our unique self, is an urgent, compelling drive of the psyche and at the same time it is sacred work.

If this work is neglected, the psyche grasps at any straw, desperately pursuing any counterfeit substitute, which holds the promise of a self. The peril is to become one of the "Hollow Men" of T.S. Elliot's great poem of that name. But even Elliot did not see how dangerous the Hollow Man is to himself and others as he props up his stunted selfhood with his arrogance, greed, lust for power and domination of others. The Hollow Man comes in a number of versions ranging from white trash and Skinheads, whose only manhood is their guns and their conviction that they are white and superior to any Black or Hispanic man.

On the other end of the social spectrum there are WASP, ivy league educated cigarette company executives and lawyers, who are convinced they have a God given right to sell high school students addictive carcinogens in order to support their fast track, high maintenance self images. In the political realm, they are the men who are convinced that there is no problem they cannot solve with power and force. These are all variations on a single theme: the false quest for the self and manhood.

The drive to create a self is there from the beginning. The photo collection, The Family of Man, has an image of a newborn infant held upside down by the birth Doctor's hand, umbilical cord still attached, the little face clenched with his first cry. The caption on the opposing page reads, "The Universe resounds with the cry, "I am."

Dr. Rollo May writes:

> The infant's capacity to cope with necessities becomes, in the growing adult, the struggle for self-esteem and for the sense of significance as a person. This...is the adult's psychological reason for living in contrast to the infant's biological one. The cry for recognition becomes the central psychological cry: "I must be able to say I AM, to affirm myself in the world."

The first chapter of Dr. Rollo May's, Power and Innocence: A Search for the Sources of Violence is entitled "Madness and Powerlessness," which begins, "Power is essential for all living things. ...The word power comes from the Latin "posse," meaning, "to be able." The prescript for Dr. May's first chapter is:

> Wherever I found the living, there I found the
> Will to power.

Thus Spake Zarathustra - Fredrich Nietzsche

Nietzsche's phrase, "the will to power", refers not to power in the sense of domination, but to the power of self-realization and being, the power to be the affirmed self. The ultimate power is the capacity to be one's unique self. Dr. May is saying that being denied our birthright of power is a source of madness: a madness that often takes the form of violence, which has its breeding ground in impotence and apathy.

May quotes Arthur M. Schlesinger, Jr.:

Indeed, no social emotion is more wide spread today than the conviction of personal powerlessness and the sense of being beset, beleaguered and persecuted. As we make people powerless, we promote their violence rather than its control. Deeds of violence in our society are performed largely by those trying to establish their self-esteem, to defend their self-image and to demonstrate that they, too, are significant. Regardless of how derailed or wrongly used these motivations may be or how destructive their expression, they are still the manifestations of positive interpersonal needs.

This is all extremely important. Schlesinger's pale, academic words "motivations" and "manifestation of positive interpersonal needs" lie over urgent drives lying deep down in the psyche. "Deeds of violence in our society are performed largely by those trying to establish their self esteem, to defend their self image and to demonstrate that they, too, are significant." These words must be read very carefully. His brilliant analysis and insight into one of the major threats to modern life: violence and crime, lies buried, ignored and forgotten in our libraries and universities. Why? Because it is demanding. It would require dedication to the creation of an authentic selfhood and to the commonweal as well. It would require taking deep responsibilities, which are foreign and uncomfortable to the immature man. Our hyper-male-dominated society is extremely adept at avoiding challenging reality and uncomfortable truth. This culture ignores challenges in the hope they will go away. We laugh at an ostrich burying its head in the sand when it feels threatened, but we don't have go to the zoo to see that.

When fundamental needs of the psyche are ignored the consequences are disastrous. The news these days, February 2002, is dominated by the fiscal free fall of the Enron Energy Corporation, a sixty billion dollar freefall. It is the largest bankruptcy in the history of the U.S. Enron stock lost 99.9%

of its value in twelve months. Thousands of investors and employees have lost their savings and retirement funds. Executives are being subpoenaed; accountants are taking the Fifth Amendment. One Enron vice chairman, Cliff Baxter, was found dead in his Mercedes with a self-inflected gunshot wound to the head. It is as bad and ugly as it ever gets on Wall Street.

The nature of Enron's collapse is stunning, not only fiscally, but also in the sheer magnitude of greed, deception, deceit and lying that was inherent to the Enron upper management and the company culture. The U.S. Congressional panel investigating Enron's collapse is issuing statements such as: "substantial evidence of illegal activity," "self dealing transactions...which violate the Internal Revenue Code and state and common law...also violates fraud statutes." Enron is rapidly becoming a case study of a corporate culture gone wrong. Clearly there is trouble in River City or more specifically, River Oaks, the very wealthy Houston neighborhood where most of Enron's top management reside. How could these quite intelligent, talented and successful men ruin their lives with these disastrous, self destructive and illegal activities? "What is wrong with these men and how did they get this way?"

The New York Times article of February 7, 2002, entitled "Darth Vader, Machiavelli, Skilling Set Intense Pace" describes the Enron C.E.O. Jeffery K. Skilling as:

> ...Creating 'a culture of risk taking.' A former Enron vice president characterized Schilling as, "You can break the rules, you can cheat, you can lie, but as long as you make money, it's all right." He told a reporter from Business Week, "I've never not been successful in business or work, ever." Another person, who worked with him at Enron, is quoted, "He didn't have a lot of respect for Washington. Schilling believes that

politicians and regulators were not as smart as he was. He's always saying people (in Washington) don't get it." (One wonders just what Skilling meant by the "it" that people "don't get."- PMH) "He was pleased and proud that people referred to him as Darth Vader."

Andrew Fastow was the Chief Financial Officer of Enron, a position he achieved at the age of thirty-six. In a twelve-month period during 2000 and 2001 he created false profits of nearly $1 billion. He is described as a "financial whiz kid" and "the Betty Crocker of cooked books". A person who worked with him at Enron said, "Mr. Fastow was adamant ...in his belief that the amount of money a person made was the only meaningful measure of success..." He used an Enron partnership to conjure a $25,000 investment into $4.5 million in two months. The special panel of the Grand Jury investigating Enron called this transaction, "especially troubling"- a masterpiece of understatement.

Fastow and the rest of these men are striving for something far greater than success. They are taking the measure of their persons, their selfhood, their very being. Neela Banerjee, in The New York Times of February, 26, 2002, wrote of Enron's corporate culture:

Everything Enron did had to be better and flashier...it celebrated Secretaries' Day with gifts of Waterford crystal -and no gesture seemed too lavish..."Extravagance by itself did not bring the company down. But the company's spending reflected a go-go corporate culture," former employees said, "in which top executives cast traditional business controls by the wayside...." "The lack of risk controls was mind boggling," said Gary Cardone, president of Dynergy Europe..." "Appearances were very important," said Jeff Gray, a former economist at Enron. "For one meeting in 1999, Enron flew in 300 of its vice presidents from around the globe to the Hyatt,

(Beaver Park, Colorado) where rooms start at $320 a night," one manager said, "It must have cost them a fortune." A $1.5 million dollar company Christmas party at Enron Field, Houston's new sports stadium, was cancelled only when Enron's bankruptcy was inevitable. Everybody flew first class. One employee, Ms. Buis, was quoted saying, "We knew we weren't making money. But the extravagance you know, is what made it great to work there."

These men went to their offices in the upper floors of the silvery blue twin towers of the Pelli designed Enron headquarters every morning totally convinced of their keen intelligence, talent and superiority. These men had invested their selfhood in this high power, high stakes, wheeling and dealing. Because this conviction was essential to their very selfhood, they had to continually prove it with greater and greater risk taking, large-scale profits and extravagant lifestyle. They were the smartest guys in the room and they were untouchable. They had to push the envelope beyond what ordinary men do; they had to run the risks to prove themselves. This is one of the tenets of the Boy Code: the willingness to take risks. This is one of the ways the men are separated from the boys.

This was the Boy Code working in the executive suite. They were players on the biggest board in town. They were on the cover of Fortune magazine. They were faster and smarter than anyone. They were bringing the NFL to the boardroom and winning was the name of the game. "Winning isn't everything; it's the only thing." It defines manhood. None of them needed the money. Fastow is married to a wealthy Houston heiress, but her money was not his money. He had to prove himself with his money. He had to take his measure.

Jean-Messier, who rode Vivendi Universal SA into the

ground for the largest loss in French corporate history with similar fiscal slight of hand. He has a self styled nickname, "J6M", short for "Jean-Marie Messier, Moi-Meme, Matrre du Monde (Jean-Marie Messier, Myself, Master of the World.) All this recalls Rollo May's earlier statement: "The cry for recognition becomes the central psychological cry: I must be able to say I AM, to affirm myself in the world."

Fastow, Skilling and Messier attempted to affirm themselves to the world and to themselves with huge financial successes, but when the affirmation of self is sought with false currency, there is never enough. It doesn't work so they keep going for more, but the affirmation never takes place. They are caught in a metaphysical Catch-22. They are caught in what Jung called, "the revenge of the unlived life," and the pursuit of a false self is, just that, an unlived life, and it had its revenge. These men and their companies were out of control.

The word "Extravagance" appears twice in Neely Banerjee's article which is defined as: "The acts of one who is not confined by any general rule, order or custom; undue expenditure of money. 2. wildness. 3. A wandering outside of proper or usual bounds." An accurate word for Enron, where traditional business principles such as, "Control the costs and the profits will take care of themselves," were thrown out the window. These men were venturing well "outside of proper or usual bounds."

Yet these men were highly intelligent, university educated in sound business principles and practices. Fastow went to Tufts, and then did an MBA at Northwestern. Skilling was a Baker scholar at Harvard Business School. But sound business principles were not controlling Enron, something else was. The go-go corporate culture of Enron was driven by a strange and ruthless energy. Skilling would command his subordinates, "Give me all the juice you can."

In her Vanity Fair article, April 2002, "The Enron Wars," Marie Brenner wrote:

> Enron, many of the women said, was a hot bed of hormones, a testosterone culture. A vice president openly displayed a "hottie board," on which he ranked the sexual allure of various Enron women.... Enron was hermitic and pulsing with sexuality. (Ironically, Playboy has propositioned several Enron women to pose for a feature on Enron's women-PMH) Ken Lay has married his secretary. Jeff Skilling had left his wife and taken up with Rebecca Carter, whom he promoted to company secretary and who earned more than $600,000 last year.
>
> (The picture in Vanity Fair of Ken Lay and his trophy wife, Linda, formerly his secretary, could well be entitled, "McGoo gets lucky."- PMH) People who know Kenneth Lay well insist that his destruction can be understood by looking at his long time attraction to ruthless, brainy alter egos such as Jeff Skilling and Andrew Fastow, who could act out Lay's ambitions while he played Mr. Congeniality. ...Skilling and Fastow allegedly designed the private partnerships that were constructed to hide losses and maximize profits....Vice presidents and managers preparing to make a budget presentation in front of Lay, Skilling and Fastow were told, "Here is your number." The number -always larger than what was feasible to demand on a contract- would have to be reached or, the vice presidents and managers knew, they could be "re-deployed, Enron language for... being forced out in a vicious biannual performance review. These performance reviews, often referred to as "rank and yank," were a variation on the old English Star Chamber.
>
> ....Skilling would be very blunt with vice presidents who questioned these methods: "Change your assumptions. You can always refinance! You can always get the deal done!"
>
> The deal structures became more and more Byzantine...Enron would sometimes swap control of its fiber lines with those of another company, only to undo the

transaction a few days later, so as to create the appearance of volume. Other manoeuvres pushed hundreds of millions of dollars of trading equity around in a circle… Young traders just out of school were tantalized with promises of $500,000 in bonuses within a year. The Enron car of choice was a silver Porsche; the parking garage in Houston was full of them…

There was occasional violence. One trader, learning that his annual bonus was a mere $500,000, was said to have thrown his $10,000 plasma screen across the trading floor. Another, fearing he would be the victim of an upcoming performance review, slammed his boss up against the wall, accusing him of lying about the trader's performance. "Forget you saw that," the man's boss told the woman who later described the event. "He's having a bad day."

According to <u>What</u> <u>Went</u> <u>Wrong</u> <u>at</u> <u>Enron:</u> <u>Everyone's</u> <u>Guide</u> <u>to</u> <u>the</u> <u>Largest</u> <u>Bankruptcy</u> <u>in</u> <u>U.S.</u> <u>History</u> by Peter C. Fusaro and Ross M. Miller, Skilling and the rest created a brutal internal corporate culture where "most employees were afraid to express their opinions or to question unethical and potentially illegal business practices."

Enron was runaway testosterone in the boardroom. They pushed the envelope to the edge and beyond until Enron became a house of cards, a flim flam pyramid investment scheme that could never hold up. The point of this examination of Enron is to understand the over the top emotional charge, the hormones, the confusion of sex and finance, the urgency and ruthlessness of it all, and to understand what was driving these men to take these high stakes, irrational risks. Risks which have destroyed their lives like gambling addicts stealing to support their habit. Enron was in the control of a collective unconsciousness, which had permeated the executive floors of Enron. To recall Grodock: these men were being lived by their unconscious, thus they were out of control and so was the company. The unconscious has little regard for logic or sound business practices. As more and more evidence of Enron's operations is uncovered, the more clearly the image of Enron emerges as a corporate culture superheated beyond endurance, emotionally, fiscally and even legally. A sting operation, which defrauded millions of people out of billions of dollars.

These men, Skilling, Fastow, Lay and the rest, proclaimed themselves "Masters of the Universe." They could push the envelope out beyond where ordinary men can go, like Chuck Yeager going for the high altitude record in his modified F-104, but in the rarefied atmosphere of 100,000 feet the flight controls didn't work and he found himself tumbling earthward with all the aerodynamics of a piece of iron pipe going end over end. He barely ejected with his life. The "Right Stuff" of test pilots is not to be confused with that of high finance and corporate responsibility. Andrew Fastow found that out when he was indicted on October 31, 2002 by the U.S. attorney for 78 counts of fraud, conspiracy, money laundering and obstruction of justice. He pleaded guilty, was contrite and cooperative. He looked stunned. His words and face seemed to say, "How could have this have happened? How could have I done this? He was granted leniency and sentenced to eight years. On May 25, 2006, Skilling and Lay were convicted on a total of nineteen charges of fraud and conspiracy. Ken Lay died of a heart attack shortly after his conviction. Skilling was sentenced to twenty four years in prison and fined 50 million.

These men have ignored Aristotle, "The definition of man is the definition of his soul." They have given their lives to a quest for a false self. A quest, which rejects the sacred work of soul-making. They have pursued a false self, an illusion. A quest, which went out of control and destroyed their lives. It a Greek tragedy set in our time. The Fifth Century Greeks knew that these matters, these sacred responsibilities are not to be taken lightly.

Years ago I took a course in Greek tragedy. It skinned my eyes like de Chardin in The Devine Milieu. The Fifth Century Greeks, Aristotle, Sophocles, Euripides, and before them, Homer, knew of a profound reality. A reality that modern man has refused to acknowledge. The great critic H.D.F. Kitto summed it up with this passage from <u>Greek Tragedy</u>:

> In the tragic vision of Sophocles, human life takes place in the midst of certain ultimates, which must be respected because they are sacred. These ultimates are life's own unbreakable laws, and within life, only half hidden, are terrible forces. These we must respect. The only saving virtue is understanding and reverence toward the ultimate claims of humanity.

The Fifth Century Greeks understood these things far better than the boys in the fraternity house. They went to the amphitheatre and the drama festivals, not for entertainment, but to catch a glimpse, an insight, into the sacred, unalterable and unwritten laws of the universe within which they had their being and their life. The Greeks knew that these fundamental ideas are not the obscure interest of some remote department of the University whose courses are best avoided and of no practical use. The Fifth Century Greeks knew that these matters constituted the bedrock of their lives, and that knowledge of these "certain ultimates," and "life's own unbreakable laws" were essential to living their lives. They went to their drama festivals, not to be entertained, but in order to learn how the universe works and the fundamental dynamics of it. They knew that these were matters not to be trifled with, not to be ignored or defied or one ends up like Creon at the end of <u>Antigone</u>.

Creon, broke the sacred law in a number of ways: first, by denying burial for the body of Polynices. He decreed, under penalty of death, that the body of Polynices was to be left outside the city walls for the dogs and carrion birds to devour. This was a terrible thing for the Greeks. The soul could not find rest with the body unburied. Antigone defies him and buries her brother. He executes her for this by walling her up in a cave. When his son, Haimon, Antigone's lover, finds Antigone's lifeless body, he tries to kill Creon, but Creon's soldiers stop him. Haimon, then, kills himself with his own sword. Eurydice, Creon's wife, learning of Haimon's suicide, poisons herself. Finally, Creon stands alone; his open hands in front of him, and speaks his last line of the play, "Everything I have touched has turned to dust."

Creon failed to respect life's own laws and terrible forces were unleashed which lashed back upon him, destroying him. Every Greek tragedy is the story of someone breaking with the sacred law, and then suffering the consequences as the energies of the Universe lash back upon him. This is what the Greeks meant by fate: our inescapable responsibility to the laws of the Universe and the consequences, which follow when they are transgressed. Ignorance of the law, rationalizations, self-justification, all count for nothing. There are no excuses - none.

To create the self is one of the tenants of the sacred law. It is both a sacred responsibility and a driving need of the psyche. These men, Skilling, Fastow and the rest, have failed to do their sacred work and the Cosmos has lashed back upon them and they are ruined. "Everything they have touched has turned to dust." To the ancient Greeks these "sacred, unalterable and unwritten laws" of the Universe had all the force and power of physical laws, all the force and power of the law of gravity or a storm at sea and they were right.

The Greek collective consciousness understood that life takes place within a great moral and metaphysical framework. Actions have inescapable consequences. These men, the executives of Enron, Global Crossing, Tycho, et al., believed there are only consequences if you are caught. If you are not caught, then it's all right and if you are clever enough, you won't get caught. Most of our society has little understanding or belief in these essential metaphysics and the forces behind them and they fail to seek any. There are exceptions: certain poets, filmmakers, writers, lovers and others living on a poetic level, who practice and affirm these realities. But in the main, we have been ignoring these forces and the laws governing them. We do so at our peril and we are in peril. Our male dominated society dismisses these concerns as not politically or economically feasible and has done so with volumes of justification. Meanwhile, every measure, which will benefit the corporate bottom line or increase the coffers of the very wealthy, passes through with ease.

We have relegated matters of the psyche, the soul, and a moral universe to the realm of Sunday morning platitudes and plaster saints on church alters. We do not see the deep needs of our souls and psyches as having any true force. We think they do not really count among the driving forces of our lives, not there on the bottom line of life.

These men, Skilling, Fastow and the rest have ignored the sacred law. But the Universe will not be denied, there is terrible power behind Dr. May's insightful line, "The cry for recognition becomes the central psychological cry: I must be able to say I AM, to affirm myself in the world." But to do this wrongly is to court disaster. Recall Virginal Sapper's words, "Any part of us that we do not accept unconditionally splits off and becomes more and more primitive...It becomes like a hungry dog in the basement." A dog, growing hungrier and hungrier, more and more primitive. These men are being lived by their unconscious, which has impelled them to take greater and greater risks until it all came down and they found themselves on the front pages of the newspapers. The false self of the macho code failed them and their lives are in ruins. The work of creating an authentic self is a sacred responsibility. This compulsive greed and power lust is just one of the manifestations of false manhood. When the work of creating an authentic self is ignored, this urgent need of the psyche is left unfulfilled. It becomes a compulsion fixating on some illusion of a self. In the case of Skilling, it was his Darth Vader persona. For the Enron corporate elite, the false self was comprised of an irresponsible, even sociopathic, brew of arrogance, ego and greed. This is the hallmark of the patriarchal man who has denied the feminine, an essential component of his selfhood. Congress with the beauty of the world and being is an essential need of the psyche.

The Ancient Greeks had a word for "A lack of experience with things beautiful." Our language has no such word. The patriarchal male has failed to cultivate any real receptivity to beauty, which he confuses with possession, and possession requires money. So it becomes all about wealth. With the men of Enron their closest contact with beauty was their silver Porches.

The Enron case is important because it reveals the widespread culture of greed lying beneath the glossy pages and opaque verbiage and accounting practices of many company annual reports. As David Rosenberg, Chief Economist and Strategist at Merrill Lynch, speaking of

Enron, said, "That's the problem with cockroaches-there is never just one.... Companies most at risk could easily fit some of the most successful companies of recent years...companies that have been hot on the acquisition trail, that have opaque financial statements, debt heavy...That cuts a pretty wide swath."

Prophetic words: not long after Rosenberg's statement the business sections of the papers were filled with the accounts of the further scandals of World Com, Global Crossing, Xerox and Tyco which have exceeded even Enron's losses. Billions more of concealed egregious losses and "accounting irregularities," a tidy euphemism for the game of hidden debits, false profits, inflated stock prices and swindled stockholders.

We are seeing a culture of mega profits, real or unreal, at any cost, at any risk. We all know what happened next: the Dow-Jones dropped nearly 2,000 points, a staggering $5.7 trillion (U.S.) in shareholder value has been wiped out and investors have pulled $18 billion out of the market. Confidence in the market has dropped to its lowest level perhaps since 1929. Allen Greenspan, chairman of the U.S. Federal Reserve, said, "An infectious greed seemed to grip much of our business community." The capitalist credo that greed is good, providing the driving force for the best of all possible economies, seems not to be working. The macho mindset of these ruthless executives is a threat to themselves, to their reputations, to their companies, to the shareholders, to the employees and finally to the fiscal health and well being of the economy and, ultimately, to us all.

These companies operating from the patriarchal ethic are often irresponsible toward the health and welfare of their employees and the environment as well. This culture of profit at any price is mortgaging the future environment and social infrastructure we are leaving to our children and grandchildren. There are huge costs to be paid down the line for the refusal of these men to be accountable.

Once again, Campbell, "We seek…the experience of being fully alive." The irresponsible executives of Enron and Global Crossing sought the "experience of being fully alive" with their super-charged, high-risk finances and lifestyles. These men choose the false self of power, domination, risk and extravagance. They listened to the hyper masculine definition of "being fully alive". They failed in their sacred work of creating a self and the Universe lashed back on them, destroying them. It is a Greek drama in our time.

Only when the self is truly served, cultivated and lived is the fullness of life achieved. The false self leaves an aching void in the psyche. A void, which can produce the irrational, self-destructive loss of reality, we see in these executives. Only the path of true self can complete the psyche. Everything else is a sham and an illusion, "A Tale told by an idiot, full of sound and fury."

CHAPTER NINE

Men, Work and the Company

Rarely do we consider work as an institution in our society. Nevertheless, it is a vital part of our culture especially for men who are the provider of the family. The patriarchal mindset is deeply entrenched in work and the company. We hear a good deal of lip service to the value of the family in our society, but very little about the importance of work in maintaining that family.

Of course, there is great concern for employment figures and work as an economic factor, but very little concern for work as a factor in the mental health and stability of men and the whole of our society. Without productive work and a humane place to do that work, a man finds it very hard to face the responsibilities of having a family. Many sociologists feel that the limited work opportunities for black men account for many leaving their families. I remember when I was out of work for a time. I felt terrible. In the morning, I would watch men going to work outside my window. They had a place to go. A place where they did something of value and received value in return. They participated in the larger work of society. I had no such participation, no such place to go. It was a very painful time in my life.

Susan Faludi in <u>Stiffed: The Betrayal of the American Male</u> understands how important work is to men. She quotes Sherwood Anderson in "Perhaps Women",

> They (men) need to touch materials with their hands. They need to form materials, need to make things with their own hands out of wood, clay, iron, etc. They need to own tools and to handle tools. Not doing it, not being permitted to do it, does something to men. They all know it That ability has "a certain power" for men and without it, 'they become no good for a woman.

In <u>Stiffed</u>, Faludi contrasts the Long Beach Naval Shipyard with McDonald Douglas Aerospace Corporation. They were both closing down and she interviewed employees from both places. She quotes Louis Rodriguez from the Shipyard saying,

> The shipyard has been a second family to me. When I get out of here, I'm really going to be lost as a whole. I will have lost my family." Ike Burr said to her, "Everything you ever dreamed of is here. The shipyard is a world within itself... There's a satisfaction in it, because you start and complete something. You see what you have created... For a man to feel he's in control of a certain situation, he has to know certain things. It is not being "in control or not in control" of people. It is having a hand in what takes place...The Bon Homme Richard was my first ship. I was in charge of putting in the cooling element foundations... What was great... was it was my first opportunity to run something, to have a vision of how something should be built that no one else had and then to go ahead and build it." When I said to management, "Do you have any idea how you want to get this done?" They said, "You tell us." Big difference.

Dennis Swan, a supervisor, spoke of the management style at the yard, "I wouldn't ask anybody to do anything I wouldn't do...People (management) need to get down to the deck plates." Like Ike Burr said, "A big difference." It is a huge difference, an empowering difference, and it paid off.

These men felt that they belonged to a company of men doing something real and important together. The yard gave them the opportunity to do men's work together with other men. The Long Beach Ship Yard with its motto, "THE SHIP, THE YARD, THE TEAM," was one of the few government facilities doing first-rate work and operating at a profit. The real reason the yard was closed down was a nasty work of politics, but that is another story for another book.

Many large corporations have several layers of middle management, which must maintain an appearance of being necessary. In order to maintain that appearance they could never have responded to Ike Burr with: "You tell us." McDonald Douglas had eleven layers of management. McDonald Douglas rewarded its workers with inflated titles and fancy nameplates and jewellery in the shape of the company's jet fighters. Out placement job counsellor, Jean Berry, told Faludi, "So many people were walking around in three piece suits calling themselves 'engineers' because McDonald Douglas called them 'engineers,' 'engineers' without an engineering degree."

When MD closed down and these men had to present their credentials and experience to another company, many of them found out that they were not really engineers after all, and they had not been doing any real work. Their resumes, as they described their jobs, were full of vague hollow words like: "expedited," "coordinated," and "facilitated." They vigorously defended the importance of what they had been doing, but they could not say for sure what it was; there was no real function there, no real job. When Berry asked one engineer "what he valued most about his years at McDonald Douglas, he launched into a detailed description of his house: $425,000 with a view! Four bedrooms! Three garages! A swimming pool and a spa! After the layoff and months of unsuccessful job searching, the $425,000 dream house "was auctioned right out from under me."

They clung to their corporate identity with the McDonald Douglas tiepins and the miniature silver airplane lapel pins, which they wore like wedding bands. The corporate culture at Douglas and then with McDonald was not healthy or productive for anyone. During 1989 – 1991, McDonald Douglas lost $344 million. G.J. Meyer, a former McDonald executive wrote in his memoir, Executive Blues, that MD's employees went "shuffling from one day to the next in a kind of low grade depression governed by an immense body of obscure rules. There were rules about everything, but most were invisible until you collided with them." For instance: it was against the company rules to jog on the property and to wear shorts." Meyer only found this out when he was reprimanded for doing just that.

Douglas Griffith told Faludi,

> You'd have a large number of the workforce standing around and they're not goofing off. For the most part, they're waiting for job assignments, because management has not empowered them to go over to the next job, which they should be able to do themselves... Half the time they are waiting for supervisors to tell them something they already know. It's the craziest system I've ever seen in my life.

Another employee said, "There was more information withheld at McDonald Douglas than any company I've ever worked for." Several other employees sitting around the table nodded in agreement. Even the trade magazine, "Aviation Week and Space Technology," commented in 1991, "Douglas essentially is operating under an authoritarian form of management."

Further, in Executive Blues, Meyers wrote, "McDouglas

was a gulag with generously compensated inmates." Don Motta said after the collapse of his life at McDonald Douglas said, "There is no way you can feel like a man.... I'll be very frank with you," he told Faludi very slowly, placing every word down as if each were an increasingly heavy weight: "I feel I've been castrated." His marriage fell apart under the strain. His wife kicked him out of the house; He lost it, kicked down a door and threatened her. Motta ended up in jail. His life had become a nightmare. A nightmare, which had its beginnings in the sick corporate culture of McDonald Douglas. The denigration and castration he had suffered at work ricocheted into his personal life. The irony here is that this dysfunctional corporate culture served not even the bottom line profitability of the company. MD destroyed the reputation of their flagship aircraft, the DC-10, when they stonewalled a problem with the cargo compartment door latch, a minor, easily fixed problem on an otherwise excellent aircraft. A problem that resulted in three crashes and nearly a thousand deaths. The DC-10 was finished and so was the Douglas Aircraft Company. For the full story on that debacle and the macho corporate culture which engineered it, see Destination Disaster by Paul Eddy.

The Lincoln Electric Company is a rare exception to the vicious and ruthless policies of the macho company. They have not laid off an employee since 1939. They have a policy they call "guaranteed employment." After a probationary period, an employee is given this status in the company. During World War II, the Office of Wage and Price Controls thought Lincoln Electric was paying their employees too much and told them to reduce their wages. The company went to the OWPC and defended their pay scale by asserting that these wages were necessary to maintain their high production. The government backed off. Lincoln did not have to do that; they would have had a perfect excuse for dropping their pay scale.

In the early eighties sales dropped off, so production had to be reduced accordingly. The standard MBA, macho, corporate response to that situation would have been to fire a large number of production workers. But Don Hastings, the president of Lincoln, did not do that. Instead, he trained his surplus manufacturing people to be salesmen and sent them out into the factories and shops that use the electric welding equipment that Lincoln manufactures. They were hands on guys and they knew how to talk to and sell these welders to shop supervisors and foremen.

Sales came back up, production came back up and so did profits. In an atmosphere like that employee morale and commitment to the company is terrific and invaluable. It affects everything: the well being of the employees and the well-being and profitability of the company. The value of this modis operandi should be obvious, but it is rarely employed. Why? Because it is foreign to the patriarchal mind which prefers dominating its people. It prefers hacking and slicing at the men in the labor force and treating them like replaceable parts in an economic machine that must be fine-tuned to run at maximum profitability. The patriarchal mind attempts to achieve this with fear and threats, power and control. They do not understand the definition of the word, "company", which is: "a group of persons who have come together for some common purpose."

The people with Lincoln Electric feel that they are valued members of a company. They feel its loyalty to them and they return it in full. They feel they are a creative part of a human enterprise, a communal, collective enterprise. These are notions with which the patriarchal mind is very uncomfortable. In the fifties, these words would have been regarded as "pinko" and "Communist." The irony was that the USSR never achieved anything like a collective communal endeavor. The worker's paradise was a vicious fascistic totalitarian regime, which more closely resembled a huge, centralized corporation than a worker's collective. It was ruthless power and control from the top down; there was nothing collective or communal about it.

Lincoln Electric still is and the Long Beach Ship Yard was a creative and productive corporate culture which respected their people and made them feel they had a voice and an input into the work and that they were regarded as workers of competence and ability and given security. With McDonald Douglas, none of this was present. MD paid the price and so did the stockholders and the employees. Everybody loses in this climate of sick masculinity in the patriarchal macho company.

CHAPTER TEN

Two Movies and a Poem

Two recent films moved me with their portrayal of the bad sex and danger of the macho mind: "Striptease," and "Eyes Wide Shut." Demi Moore's' "Striptease" reveals the empty, obsessive and destructive nature of the patriarchal male's projection and obsessive sexuality. "Striptease" is an uncomfortable film about a woman, played by Demi Moore, who is economically trapped into the sexual exploitation of stripping in order to support herself and her young daughter. It is painful to watch her exposing herself to the howling louts who comprise her audiences. Her humiliation is compounded when her daughter accidentally sees her perform. Then the Burt Renolds' character, a besotted, lecherous, old senator, becomes obsessed with her. He is pathetic, but, at the same time, dangerous, as he contrives to trap and rape her aboard a yacht. He is convinced of his male entitlement to possess her. The film shows how bent and warped the patriarchal psyche can become with its projection and obsession. The film was greatly underestimated by the critics, who, I suspect, could barely sit through the pain, humiliation and danger Demi Moore's character had to endure, as well as the sheer insanity of the obsessive sex spawned in the imagination and macho sexuality of the Senator.

Stanley Kubrick's, "Eyes Wide Shut" is another underestimated, interesting and complex film exploring the dark side of sex when love is denied. It is the story of one couple's passage through the labyrinth created by sex of the imagination, sex apart from love and relationship. Michael Herr in his brilliant Vanity Fair, November 2000, piece, "Completely Missing Kubrick," writes:

> Stanley was in the mood for love, he made a movie that was all for love...about a couple crossing that sector of the connubial minefield where the devices are especially well buried... He turned his gaze upon a conjugal arrangement composed of trust and complacency in equal measure, which is to be tested in the fire.

The trial by fire begins at the party where a tantalizing young creature, Nuala, asks Tom Cruise's character, Dr. Bill Hartford, "Don't you want to go where the rainbow ends?" and it is clear that the rainbow Nuala and her equally fetching little buddy, Gayle, have in mind is bedding down with the two of them. However, at that moment, Hartford is summoned by his wealthy host to medically administer to a nude female guest who has overdosed on a brew of coke and heroin.

After the party, Dr. Bill and his wife, Alice, go home and smoke a joint together. Alice confronts Bill on the two girls he was talking to at the party. She is a little loopy from the joint and accuses him of wanting to f -- k them. She doesn't believe his denial nor will she let up on him as she bores in on him, "Let's say for example you have some gorgeous woman standing in your office naked, and you are feeling her f--king tits. Now what I want to know is: What are you thinking while you are squeezing them?"

He insists that he is a doctor and nothing else is going on, but she won't stop, "And what do you think she is thinking about handsome Doctor Bill?" He answers, "Women aren't like that." She doubles up with laughter as she replies, "If you men only knew." She tells him about last summer at

Cape Cod when she saw a young naval officer, "He glanced at me. I could hardly move. If he wanted me even if for just one night I was ready to give up everything, you, Helena (their daughter), my whole fucking future, everything... and yet at the same time you were dearer to me than ever."

Hartford is stunned, the phone rings and he is called out on the death of a friend and patient. He cannot get the image of Alice having sex with the naval officer out of his mind. He finds himself in a sexually charged New York City nightscape wandering from one erotic episode to another as if in a dream.

He runs into an old friend from school playing piano at a cocktail lounge who tells him about playing for these strange wealthy parties. He gives Hartford the address and password for the party that night and instructs him to wear a black cape and mask. After a visit to a costume shop, Hartford takes a cab to the address, which is a huge estate with a guarded gate. He is asked for the password which admits him into a large house, which resembles a dark cathedral. It is filled with people wandering around wearing masks and dark ritualistic robes except for some of the women, who are nude and beautiful as models. They wander like masked mannequins in a dim underworld. There is no warmth not even around the couples who are copulating some of whom are women with women. There is a feeling of a dark and sombre ritual taking place.

Hartford is mysteriously recognized by one of the nude women. She tells him he is in danger and must leave, but he stays. Soon after he escorted to a huge room where he is encircled by all those present. He has been found out as an intruder and condemned to death. But the woman who warned him offers her life for his and he is permitted to leave by some strange dispensation. All this has the quality of a dark dream, but then "Eyes Wide Shut" is a dream movie, about the dark waking dream that many live out around sex.

We catch a glimpse of the empty reaches of this dark sexuality as Victor, Hartford's rich friend, speaks of the woman at his party, "The one with the great tits who O.D.ed in my bathroom." That is all women are to these men: great tits, great ass, great looks, great body. Their orgy is a ritualistic celebration of faceless, autonomous, phantasmagorical sex, sex of the imagination. The dark sexuality of these men who use sex in an attempt to replenish themselves and to restore their own emptiness as they drain energy from their sex. It is sex as horrific usage. The Casanovas of the world use women like this. They are the connoisseurs of sex and women, but they have no sense, whatsoever, of the vision of sex and love, D.H. Lawrence had as he wrote:

> Sex, to me, means the whole of the relationship between man and woman. And the relation of man to woman is wide as all life. It consists in infinite different, flows between the two beings...an infinite range of subtle communication of which we know nothing about...The relation of man to woman is the flowing of two rivers side by side, sometimes even mingling, then separating again, and traveling on... this is the flow of living sex, the relation between man and woman...

Lawrence is speaking here of the subtle energetic exchange which runs through a genuine sexual relationship which at the same time is much larger than sex because their sex is a celebration of their relationship and of life itself.

One critic called "Eyes Wide Shut" "a series of erotic misadventures," which it is, but that critic missed the point that these truly are misadventures, nightmarish misadventures. They are neither sensual nor erotic; they are counterfeit and empty. These unreal misadventures deny the real sexuality and eroticism of committed true relationship. They are nothing and that irony is the real action of the film. The point of the movie is that Hartford and Alice come to realize the emptiness of these misadventures and they choose to recreate their relationship instead.

But "Eyes Wide Shut" was a flop at both the box office and with many of the critics. They came expecting a "fuckorama" (Herr's great term) with two of the current cinema's superstars. Instead they got some hard damage done to their fantasies of orgy sex with beautiful strangers, like going to "Where the rainbow ends" with a couple of nymphets like Nuala and Gayle. They didn't like it much.

Bill and Alice come to reject all this for the sake of what they have together. Every time we saw them together, they were deeply enmeshed in the mundane details of domesticity: their daughter's homework, social engagements, Christmas shopping, commitments, etc., the dishwater of everyday life and everyday relationship. The first time we see them they are in the bathroom; she is on the toilet. It is a long way from the end of the rainbow with those two little gals. Alice asks him, "Do I look all right?" Without looking at her, he answers, "You look perfect." He doesn't have to look; he knows she looks perfect. She always looks perfect.

In the last scenes of the film, Hartford comes home, looks in on his sleeping daughter, walks into his bedroom to see Alice asleep and on the pillow next to her is his mask from the orgy. He had not been able to find it when he returned the costume. He is horrified; he breaks down weeping. She wakes, he holds her as he says through his tears, "I'll tell you everything." The camera cuts to Alice's face after she has heard it all. After a long moment, she says, "Helena will be up. She is expecting us to take her Christmas shopping," and they are occupied with the demands and everyday routine of their marriage. At the shopping mall they have a moment together and knowing that his marriage and his life is hanging in the balance, Bill asks her,

"Alice, what do you think we should do?

"Maybe," She answers, after a long moment, "I think we should be grateful that we have survived through all our adventures whether they were real or only a dream in the long night of a whole lifetime."

"No dream is just a dream." He answers.

"The important thing is we are awake now and, hopefully, for a long time to come. I do love you and there is something we need to do as soon as possible."

In very direct language, she tells him what it is they must do, and then they proceed home to do just that. With their sexual love, they will renew their relationship and pledge their love and sexuality to one another. With this pledge, the curse is lifted. They have renounced the sexual confusion and shimmering unreality of these last few days. They have chosen the "living sex" of which Lawrence spoke. They have chosen love and relationship with all its ordinariness. They forgive themselves and each other. They have chosen each other, frailties included, and sexual frailty is the most difficult of all to accept. As Alice says, "The important thing is we are awake now..." they have chosen the path of conscious real love as opposed to the trance and dream sexuality of illusion and meaningless misadventures. Now they are going home to make love and renew their relationship and their commitment to each other. Their sex becomes a bond and pledge, each to the other. They have chosen to love a real person, their partner, not an illusion created in their imagination. With their choice, they have survived the labyrinth of unreal sex and unlived life.

So "Eyes Wide Shut" is a profound love story with a happy ending, albeit hard won, and a very close call. Not an easy story to tell and hardly the "fuckorama" with two beautiful super stars, Nichole Kidman and Tom Cruise, that a number of people and critics came to see and which the film promotion hinted at. They came for an erotic film, but "Eyes" was about the failure of Victor and his rich friends to achieve an erotic life because they have no faith in the rich possibilities of relationship and sexuality spoken of by Lawrence. Instead, they have chosen to pursue a dark, strange, vicarious sexuality. They are lost in a bizarre labyrinth deep within their own psyches.

At a screening in Orangeville, Ontario, a disappointed patron stood up and said, "I thought we were going to see Cruise and Kidman have sex." Instead they got a dead serious movie about love, sex and its pitfalls: like the soul eating lack of trust and jealousy that Hartford suffered over Alice's fantasy over the young naval officer and the temptation of going to the "end of the rainbow" with Nuala and Gayle, a fantasy held near and dear by many men as well as the fascination of a perverse orgy of group sex. But, truth and reality on this level are seldom popular and so this film never got the attention it deserved. Granted, "Eyes" is very complex, hardly an easy, pleasant or entertaining tale and it has cinematic difficulties; Kubrick died before he could finish it, so it had to be finished and edited by someone else. Nevertheless, Stanley was clearly about something profoundly ambitious and necessary; it deserves our close attention. One of the few critics who understood "Eyes" was Janet Maslin in The New York Times. Maybe it takes a woman to know a love story when she sees one.

Ironically, two weeks after I wrote this piece on "Eyes Wide Shut," the Cruise Kidman marriage has blown up over the very issues the film was dealing with: jealousy, accusations of infidelity, insecurity and doubt. Any relationship has mysterious depths and issues of which the participants themselves are scarcely aware, but, from the accounts of conversations between them, all of the above issues seemed to be there. Perhaps they would benefit from watching the film again very closely.

The critics, most of whom were male, generally reviewed both films badly. Sexuality is an unresolved matter for the collective male psyche and, hence, uncomfortable, but these films are valuable. They offer a visceral portrayal of these powerful psycho dynamics. When the deep needs of the soul are neglected, there are consequences. C.S. Jung spoke of "the revenge of the unlived life." These are not the idle speculations of academics, but huge psychic forces, which cannot be ignored. They will not go away. The failure to love truly is one of the ways we fail to live our lives. When men fail to love, that deep need for love goes terribly foul. It rots the soul. The Duke in Richard Browning's poem, "My Last Duchess" is such a man.

"My Last Duchess" dramatizes the smouldering fury of the patriarchal psyche when a woman fails to live up to his unreal demands and expectations. The poem opens with the Duke showing a visitor his palace and art collection:

> That's my last Duchess painted on the wall,
> Looking as if she were alive. I call
> That piece a wonder now; Fra Pandolf's hands
> Worked busily a day and there she stands."

The Duke goes on to speak of "The depth and passion of its earnest glance," and "that spot of joy" on her cheek. Then he asks,

How such a glance came there...
Sir, t'was not her husband's presence only, called that
spot of joy into the Duchess' cheek; Perhaps
Fra Pandolf chanced to say......'Paint
Must never hope to reproduce the faint
Half flush that dies along her throat:'

His complement was,
                cause enough
For calling up that spot of joy. She had
          A heart, how shall I say? Too soon made glad
Too easily impressed: she liked whatev'er
She looked on, and her looks went everywhere.
Sir, t'was all one! My favor at her breast...
The bough of cherries some officious fool
Broke in the orchard for her, the white mule
She rode around the terrace all and each
Would draw from her alike the approving speech
                    Or blush
Somehow, I know not how as if she ranked
My gift of a nine hundred years old name
                With anyone's gift.

But he was not one to "stoop to blame" "this sort of trifling," not one to instruct her because:

E'en then would be some stooping; and I choose
Never to stoop. Oh sir, she smiled, no doubt
Whene'er I passed her; but who passed without
Much the same smile? This grew; I gave commands;
Then all smiles stopped together. There she stands
                As if alive.

Then they are to "meet the company below". On the way down, he points out another of his works of art:

Notice Neptune, though
Taming a sea horse, thought a rarity,
Which Claus of Innsbruck cast in bronze for me!

His jealousy and lust requires that he totally possess her, that she is his and his alone. His frustration in this so enrages him that he has her killed, and now he has what he wanted from the beginning: a work of art for his collection to which he alone possesses and has access. The portrait of her has a curtain in front of it, which he alone draws. The horror of the poem is increased by the Duke's tone, which implies that there is nothing extraordinary in what he has done, that his actions were a natural and understandable response.

The final horror of the poem is that "the company below" includes the Count with whom the Duke is negotiating another marriage to, and there is little doubt that this horror will continue with this unfortunate, beautiful, young woman, who is about to become another object d'art in the Duke's collection.

CHAPTER ELEVEN

Love: What it is; What it isn't

"No land in human topography
     is less explored than that of love."

Ortega y Gasset

"Falling in love" is an interesting phrase; it implies an encounter with a force beyond our control, like gravity. The romantic in us feels insulted by these discussions of the projections, fantasies, and illusions we create out of our need for love. Our shimmering hopes feel like the richest possibility that life has to offer. I remember my philosophy professor, Dr. Dewart, at the University of Toronto, in one of his lectures:

> I've just got to say this: most of you will fall in love and marry. Six months or a year later, you will wake up in bed with your partner look over at them and realize that you have married a complete stranger. Then you will have to decide whether you are going to walk out of the relationship or come to know and love this person you are in bed with.

We could feel that he was speaking from an intense personal experience that he wanted to pass it on to us.

Ethel Person, in <u>Dreams of Love and Fateful</u>

Encounters, writes of falling in love:

> The lover thinks his love is aroused solely by the virtues of the loved one. It will not help to tell him that this is an illusion, that it is he who has endowed the beloved with so much value. Outsiders say that beauty is in the eye of the beholder, that love is a projection, but the lover feels enthralled by what he believes to be the actual attributes of the beloved. The lover (knowing nothing of the existence of the Lover Shadow-PMH) invariably attributes his love to the loved ones specialness, not to the creative powers of his imagination.

My brother Ken sensed all this when I once said of a lady friend, "Susan is wonderful." He responded, "No one is wonderful." He knew I was vulnerable to just this sort of romantic projection, and he was right. Shakespeare saw through the illusion with great lucidity as he has Duke Theseus say, "The lunatic, the lover, the poet are of imagination all compact." In saying so, his Duke Theseus both celebrates and mocks the act of the imagination we call "falling in love." An interesting phrase, "both celebrates and mocks."

We need a completely new approach to intimate relationships, to creating intimate relationships. The very notion that relationships are created is an important beginning and a letting go of the fantasy that it is something that magically happens to us like it does in the song from "South Pacific,"

> Some enchanted evening
> You will see a stranger
> You will see a stranger
> Across a crowded room
> And somehow, you'll know
> You'll know even then

You will see him again and again

Our culture is filled with this celebration of projection and fantasy, which is exactly what, is happening across that crowded room with the stranger. Our culture believes that this is love and this is how it happens and it is just a matter of finding the right person with the right "juice" as a lady I know puts it. A lady who has been through three marriages and three divorces and now a grandmother at fifty two, she still pursues the fantasy of that enchanted evening with a stranger across the room or the tennis club or wherever. Many of us are addicted, God knows I was, to the magical hope that these fantasies seem to hold, but they consume our lives and keep us from the possibilities for life and love that are present in our lives.

John Welwood writes, "The dream of love distracts us from the path of love." The dream of love is the projection and shimmering illusion that the right love will heal us, make us whole and finally fully alive. These fantasies and projections of ours are our waking dreams and trances and like our dreams when we are asleep, we think they are reality. The power of this phantasmagoria is vastly underestimated. We all think, "I could never be this crazy." Unfortunately, most of us underestimate our capacity for craziness. I did for a long time.

Our cultural mainstream understands little about creating love and relationship. Committed inner work is required. The beginning of most relationships is like jumping into the deep end of the pool before taking swimming lessons.

But deep down in our culture, down below this overlay of unreality, we begin to hear phrases like "conscious loving" coming from people like Harvile Hendricks and John

Welwood. They talk of loving with awareness and consciousness as opposed to blindly following the siren calls of projection, illusion and fantasy. Loving, with the awareness that intimacy will stir up the old stuff, loving with a readiness to work with that challenge and to do the inner work around that challenge. Loving that accepts the reality that there is no easy way.

If we feel jealous, angry, obsessive or any one of the whole gamut of feelings that can come up in a relationship, we must recognize that these feelings are symptoms of the work that needs to be done if we are to be in loving relationship. If we truly love our partner and are truly committed to this relationship this is what it takes. A conscious loving partner will accept these feelings as a challenge and a necessity to heal and to develop greater self-awareness, compassion and spiritual growth. The stakes are high. The challenge is to become more fully who we are as we take on the turbulent waters of sex and relationship. The feminine understands these things more readily than the masculine.

However, the macho male wants none of this, he wants to use the energies of love and sex to satisfy himself. The operative word is use, usage. The feminine consciousness intuitively understands that these energies have a higher potential of serving relationship and life. As a culture, we must give this feminine consciousness priority, and make help acceptable and available. The patriarchal mind will oppose this work. It prefers to act out the feelings and eliminate the challenges with power, control, domination and denial because it knows this inner work is the realm of the feminine. A realm it does not know; nor does it want to know. The patriarchal mind does not give ground easily. Being involved with a man dominated by this mind set is extremely difficult because he will respond with fury to the inevitable challenges of a relationship.

How do we avoid being trapped in such a relationship? First, we must understand the patriarchal mind and how it responds to relationship and challenge. Then, as a friend of mine does, she asks the guy early in the relationship, "Well, what are we doing here? Are we just entertaining ourselves or are we looking at the possibility of serious relationship? I've got enough friends in my life. I'm looking for serious relationship." She says, "This rocks some guys back but it sorts them out, and I know where they stand"- a smart lady.

Then you start talking about what a real relationship is all about and how it works. Then, if he is still around, you start reading Hendricks and Welwood together and you begin to practice the communication and openness that a real relationship requires. If he is the right kind of guy, he will be interested. If he is not, he will be gone and you will know he is not worth your time. Granted, this is not easy and it takes confidence and courage, but it is far better than having your guts and your life torn up by some guy who is incapable of relationship; a man who is impossible.

Intimate relationship is a crucible, "A smithy of the soul," in which the self is forged and refined. My friend is saying to these men, "If you don't want the heat, get out of my kitchen." The last time I saw her she looked very happy with her gentleman friend.

Confusion between love and projection permeates our culture. We have become addicted to all the fantasy, drama, adrenalin and the racing heart that goes with the projection. We have become a society of romance junkies. A good many of our songs about love reflect this addiction. For instance, Smokey Robinson's, "You Really Got a Hold on Me".

I don't like you, but I love you,
Seems that I'm always thinking of you
Though you treat me badly,
I love you madly,
You really got a hold on me.

This is not love, not the joy of mutual love and affection. It is addiction. Another revealing song is Al Hamilton's "I've Got to Have You."

I need your love to survive,
Without it, I'm just half-alive,
I'm forgetting all my pride,
I couldn't leave you, girl, if I tried

There it is, the emptiness and dependence that accompanies the projected anima, not the fullness of one's self in love. "Need," "survive," "just half alive," the language could not be stronger or more descriptive of the agony that accompanies the stunted self in projection. The problem is that the emotional roller coaster ride of the love junkie can turn very nasty because if the relationship dies, the love junkie finds the existential rug pulled out from under him. Suddenly, his life has no hope, no prospects for joy or love. Some men turn on the woman who has done this to him with the blind fury of an outraged child. At this point, anything can happen. These are the emotions, which were churning the guts and psyches of O.J. Simpson, Hunter S. Thompson, Frank Sinatra and thousands of other men who have stalked, beaten and even murdered their partners.

Much of D.H. Lawrence's writing was about the dynamics which take place between men and women. In Women In Love, he wrote: "Man must be considered as a broken off fragment of a woman and sex was the still aching scar of the wound Man must be added on to a woman, before he had any real place or wholeness."

I believe Lawrence is using the word "woman" in this passage to refer to the feminine. Again, the notion of wholeness appears. In the previous chapter, we read Lawrence's great passage on "The flow of living sex." In Women in Love, he writes of a "void" and a certain lack:

> She always felt vulnerable, vulnerable; there was always a secret chink in her armor. She did not know herself what it was. It was the lack of a robust self, she had no natural sufficiency there was a terrible void, a lack, a deficiency of being within herself. And she wanted someone to close it up...close it up forever.

Lawrence is writing of a female character here, but he knew that the same void and vulnerability is present in men as well. In The Plumed Serpent, he wrote, "Oh, if there is one thing men need to learn...it is to collect each man his own soul deep inside him, and to abide with it."

In this poetic passage, we hear echoes of Teihard Chardin. Insight which O.J. Simpson and the rest never heard of because it is not there in the macho culture. Love addicts are addicted to the intense emotional rush of infatuation which is the yearning, driving hope that SHE will fill and satisfy all the old need for love and warmth which was not there long ago when we so needed it. The hope that she will fill the void, which lies there, deep inside, like some black hole and all that need and hope is confused with love.

What is not there is an understanding of what love truly is. Again, in The Plumed Serpent, Lawrence wrote, "What love requires is time, shared experiences and feelings, mutual caring and acceptance and a long and tempered bond between two people."

In Women in Love, he wrote, "What I want with you is a strange conjunction,' he said quietly; 'not a mingling you are quite right: ...but an equilibrium, a pure balance of two single beings as stars balance each other."

Lawrence is talking here about a relationship of balance between two equals without dependency, without addiction, without compulsive need, a state of joy, not one of anxious dependency. Naturally, with a loving relationship there is a desire to be with the one you love, but that desire is far different from the raging dependent need of a projection.

With love, the desire is to know the other, to be with the beloved, to create relationship. With a projection, there is only the need of how she makes him feel, the need of how she completes him, of how she fills the emptiness within and because the need is desperate, the only security is possession and control of her. She is a vital accessory to his life, but there is no shared life, of his life with her, or of her life with him. All he wants is her to act out the role assigned to her by his projection and if she steps out of that role, he is threatened, anxious and, very likely, furious.

Knowing the difference between love and projection with these men is not always easy, because during courtship they are on their best behavior as they attempt to seduce the woman into their notion of a relationship, which is closer to usage than relationship. Time and the inevitable challenges of a relationship are the only tests we have. Only in time can we achieve this, of which John Welwood writes,

> Conscious love begins to develop in a relationship where two people share a being-to-being communion. It is a love of being rather than a love of personality. In moments of communion, I am in touch with the depth of my own being and my partner's being at the same time... I become as

sensitive to her longings and cannot separate myself from her pain. We have interpenetrated too deeply for me ever to be able to stand entirely separate from her again.

This is not easy stuff. Many relationships go on the rocks because one or both partners just do not have the consciousness or the will or the capacity to go there. Eric Fromm, in The Art of Loving, writes:

Mature love is union under the condition of preserving one's integrity, one's individuality. It is the union of two persons standing as whole and secure persons.

It is a state of intensity, awakeness, enhanced vitality, which is at the same time a productive, creative, active engagement in many other spheres of life. The lovers manifest an active concern for the life and growth of both the beloved and all that is loved.

Unless we love from this state and have faith in the substance of ourselves, our sense of identity is threatened, and we become dependent on someone else, a lover, whose love and approval becomes the basis for our identity.

Jalaja Bonheim asked her friends, "What does sacred sexuality mean to you?" Roseanne answered, "...It's like a great light... Life comes pouring into existence..." Janet said, "Sex is the light that streams from the body." Another said, "Sex is magic. It's a field of magic...It's the primal creative force. It moves through you, but it doesn't belong to you; you can't possess it."

Bonheim quotes Sobonfu Some, a teacher from the African Dagara tribe, "Her language has no words for having sex. The equivalent Dagara phrase translates as "going on a journey together," a journey guided by the spirits of the ancestors. A journey by which the human and spirit worlds of the whole village are brought into alignment. Bonheim quotes the ancient Greeks calling Aphrodite, the "laughter

loving goddess," who was always surrounded by children."
"Sex is one of the most potent spiritual teachers we will ever
encounter." This sort of luminous consciousness of the
possibilities of sex is far beyond our ordinary consensus, but
most of us sense it and hope for it. Only with determination
and will, can we create this level of love and sexual union.
Fantasy and projection will not serve.

Erica Jong's <u>Fear of Flying</u> wrestles with all these issues.
After five years of a marriage, which feels to her like "So
many years of being half of something (like the back two legs
of a horse outfit on a vaudeville stage)," she wants to know if
she is still whole and she is itchy for romance and new sex.
She dreams of the "Zipless Fuck."

> The zipless fuck was more than a fuck. It was a Platonic
> ideal. Zipless because when you came together zippers fell
> away like rose petals, underwear blew off in one breath like
> dandelion fluff. Tongues intertwined and turned liquid. Your
> whole soul flowed out through your tongue and into the
> mouth of your lover.
>
> For the true, ultimate zipless A 1 fuck, it was necessary
> that you never get to know the man very well...there is no talk
> at all. The zipless fuck is absolutely pure... I had noticed for
> example how all my infatuations dissolved as soon as I really
> became friends with a man, became sympathetic to his
> problems, listened to him kvetch about his wife, or ex wives,
> his mother, and his children. After that I would like him,
> perhaps even love him but without passion. And it was
> passion that I wanted.... I no longer dreamed about him. He
> had a face. The zipless fuck is the purest thing there is. And it
> is rarer than a unicorn. And I have never had one. Whenever
> it seemed I was close, I discovered a horse with a paper mache
> horn...Alessandro, my Florentine friend, came close. But he
> was, after all, one clown in a unicorn suit.

This is passion of the imagination, a home movie inside

one's own head, which is interrupted with the presence of a real person. Once "he had a face," it was all over. Then she reminisces back to her teens and twenties:

> So the search for the impossible man went on...any one of my many shrinks could tell you that I was looking for my father...Not that it seemed wrong; it just seemed too simple...Perhaps it was a kind of quest. Perhaps there was no man at all, but just a mirage conjured by our longing and emptiness...
>
> Maybe the impossible man was nothing more than a spectre made of our own yearning.

Jong is brilliant here. Our quest for The Magic Princess Fairy Godmother or Mr. Right Juices or Mr. /Miss Wonderful is a quest for a myth of our own making, a mirage of our own creation.

But Isodora did not know that yet, so when Adrian Goodlove came along and told her, "You've a lovely ass," she was more than ready. They have a brief bantering conversation, and "Adrian kept grinning. Both of us knew I had finally met the real zipless fuck."

Bennett, her husband, knew exactly what was going on as he said, "If you're in love with him why don't you commit yourself to it and meet his kids in London. But you can't even do that. You don't know what you want." She admits to herself, "Adrian was a dream. Bennett was my reality." Still the next day she is with Adrian lying on a blanket in the Vienna woods, while he proposes a madcap jaunt through Europe along with some fast talk about fun, freedom and no guilt. "And meanwhile," he says, "We'll have a great time." Later, as she reflects on all this, "I tried to tell myself I was hurting Bennett, hurting myself, making a spectacle of myself. I was. But nothing helped. I was possessed. The minute he walked into a room and smiled at me, I was a goner."

So she leaves Bennett and takes off with Adrian in his Triumph across Europe in pursuit of the zipless fuck. There is a lot of high IQ talk about sex and life. Then driving through the Alps with the top down, Adrian tells her "In the mornings, I never can remember your name," which should have told her something about what was going to happen next. Namely that he would return to his wife and kids in England, and that she has been nothing but a casual diversion. She begins to understand that this whole trip has been nothing but desperation and depression masquerading as freedom. After Adrian's betrayal and usage of her, she realizes that all her feelings for him had been a product of "the creative powers of her imagination." She does some serious thinking about sex, life and relationship and the emptiness inside her that she has been trying to fill, "...what I had originally wanted. A man to complete me... But perhaps that was the most delusional of all my delusions. People don't complete us. We complete ourselves. If we haven't the power to complete ourselves, the search for love becomes a search for self annihilation and then we try to convince ourselves that self annihilation is love."

Isadora has it right here. She wants to see Bennett, not to fall back into what they had in the past because that didn't work, but to see if something new, more real and fuller than what they had in the past can now be created. She goes to London, finds his hotel, but he is not in. She gets the key from the room clerk. She is taking a bath as Bennett walks in and the novel ends at that point.

We do not know what happens next but we have a sense that she offered him the possibility and the hope of something quite new. A new and different relationship and he would have to decide whether or not to embark on that.

She knows that she has been looking for the wrong things in love. She knows now that living and loving is being born over and over again. But whatever the outcome with Bennett, she is not afraid. She takes her life back as she renounces the fantasy of the zipless fuck. It doesn't exist. Now she goes forth to explore the topography of love and of her own soul. She has come a long way, and it has not been easy. I just hope that I have arrived at the point were she is now.

CHAPTER TWELVE

A Belly Full of Snakes: Hunter with Sandy

Hunter S. Thompson is one of my favorite writers, a wild, comic, crazy, but at the same time, insightful man. When I picked up Jean Carroll's brilliant <u>Hunter: The Strange and Savage Life of Hunter S. Thompson</u>, I couldn't put it down. Hunter's relationship his wife, Sandra Dawn Thompson Tarlo, is a sad tale of love and terrible wounding. It tells a lot about the destructive power of these unconscious dynamics and projections operating within a relationship. It is a tale of a man totally crippled in his ability to love and relate to a woman.

Hunter and Sandy were so in love. She talked about Hunter to Jean Carroll:

> ...The first time I really saw him was in a basement apartment in the Village. Standing in the doorway. Hunter loomed in under it in his madras shorts and white alligator shirt. And he had a big thick manuscript under his arm. And he stood there in the doorway. He hadn't said a word. And I remember I was in this little alcove bed thing. Lying on the bed... And I looked at Hunter in the doorway and I was gone. My heart just leaped out of my body." Then later, "... he asked to meet me for a drink. My heart just raced... We met at that same bar on Christopher Street. We were just absolutely smitten. Just drinking away, getting drunker and more and more attracted. He wanted me to come up to the cabin with him that night. But I said I had to be with my father at his new house on Long Island and help decorate the tree. I took

the last train, which was at eleven. The whole way out there I was just flying on the train. I stood between the cars, outside, and I don't believe I have ever been higher in my life...Then he called me a couple days before New Year's Eve. Three o' clock in the morning. I should have known right then! He said, "I'm coming to the city. Would you like to get together?" He came to my apartment. We just fell into each other's arms. We spent four or five days in my single bed in my teeny bedroom ...wrapped around each other. I was so happy and he was so happy.

But then the first sign of trouble, on their honeymoon in Puerto Rico,

We were in our little house with the big screen window right at the edge of the water. In the jungle. It was total jungle all around us. There were birds and little lizards.

One day I went for a walk on the beach. Hunter was swimming. And I walked down the beach and around a bend. All of a sudden, I heard screaming. It was Hunter.

Of course I came running back, and he cried, "Don't ever do that again! Never get out of my sight again!" And he threw his arms around me....

Then he'd go out and chop coconuts, and we'd eat the coconuts and we'd have coconut rum drinks and then he would carve them. He had a whole row on the wall of carved coconuts.

And we'd make love. There was a big screen and we were right on the ocean, the sand and the ocean, and I remember I was sitting up and we were in bed and I just thought I can't get any higher. If I were to die in the next instant, I would be happy.

But then a little later there was an even greater sign of danger,

But there was an incident...after we came back from Bermuda to New York...a friend of Hunter's and his wife asked us for cocktails and dinner and to spend the night. We all talked and drank and then I remember going into the kitchen and the husband was there and we got into my favorite and only conversation for years and years. We talked about Hunter, this amazing man.

When I came out of the kitchen. Hunter had left the living room. I went upstairs to our room. It was dark and the bed was on the floor. I knelt down on the bed and all of a sudden, out of nowhere came this really powerful punch across my face. I was instantly in shock. What I saw was for reasons unknown to me, my very high and loving and wild life with this amazing man was over. My world had ended! That pain far superseded any physical pain. It never occurred to me that he was crazy or violent and that I didn't deserve it. Of course, he was jealous and after a lot of sobbing and crying, I "realized" that it was all a "miscommunication."

How very, very sad. As Sandra recalls her life with Hunter to Jean Carroll, we see the signs of danger. We feel his desperate need of her, which creates a fear of losing her. The power of this fear creates an unreality in his mind that it is actually happening and that she is coming on to other men. Convinced of his inner unreality, he is enraged and beats her. Ultimately, his need and fear will drive the love of his life away. Ultimately, such men, their guts churning with fear and vulnerability are compelled to dominate, overpower and possess their women. They must diminish the woman's power and individuality. This can never be love; it drives out love. The blind power of their need and vulnerability drives out and kills the love they so desperately need.

Men like Hunter need the woman so deeply that it is impossible for them to feel secure. The power of their insecurity begins to generate its own reality; "I feel so tortured and insecure that she must actually be unfaithful and unloving." This is "delusional jealousy." This kind of insecurity chews at a man's guts and churns out these horrible unrealities. A character in Norman Mailer's novel, An American Dream, said it all with the line: "My belly was a pit of snakes." It is all a painful and terrible irony. Hunter beats her for talking to another man about how much she loves Hunter. Then he is too defensive to talk about it with anyone or to get help with the feelings tearing at his gut. These men scorn the idea of therapy or even talking about what they are feeling. All that is for wimps.

The more insecure a person is, the more defensive they are about their version of reality and any suggestion that they might not be seeing things clearly, or that they might need help with a relationship. Their scorn of therapy and of in depth communication is another danger signal. Sandra's word, "miscommunication", is in quotes probably because it was Hunter's word, but this was far more than a miscommunication. It was Hunter's rational for the craziness and unreality raging in his mind, which overpowered him and drove him to beat the woman he so loved. He tried to scale down the ugly craziness of what has happened to a mere "miscommunication" which in his mind was partially Sandra's fault for not communicating and thus creating the situation.

This is all very sad, destructive and tragic. When this kind of unreality appears in a relationship, it is another serious danger signal, which cannot to be ignored. Sandy said, "It never occurred to me that he was crazy..." If crazy is defined as acting on a distorted inner mental state rather than reality, then men like Hunter, at times like this, are momentarily crazy. The legal and medical definitions are not useful here. Sandra has also quoted the word "realized" probably because Hunter demanded that she go along with his warped version of what actually took place. She consented because she knew nothing else was possible with

Hunter. She loved him so, and this was the price Hunter demanded.

But it didn't stop there. Again, in Sandra's words to Jean Carroll:

> There were beatings. Maybe six after the first heavy wallop when we were first together... I was going to the health club and I didn't want the other women to see that I had been beaten...I didn't want them to know that Hunter had done this.
>
> So I was protecting Hunter. It wasn't a matter of how I looked, that I was the kind of person who could be beaten. It wasn't that. It was that I was protecting Hunter...One of those times I hit him back. Yeah, good. Except I just got hit a little harder. I was not much of a match... Hunter beat me. OK. Not good. OK. Next chapter.

With these men, their first act of violence is seldom the last. That first instance is a symptom of a serious imbalance, which is not going to go away on its own. Nicholas von Hoffman, a friend of them both, said, "For Hunter to wreck that marriage took a lot of work." Yes, a lot of work and a lot of craziness.

Another way these men control their women is with ironclad routines and schedules. Hunter's routine was to stay up all night until 6 AM, then sleep until 3 PM. Sandy recalled what it was like:

> He would count on me to get him up. And I'd go in, and in this little, little voice, I'd kneel next to the bed and I'd say, "Hunter, it's time to get up." And he'd go, "Ohhh, mmmmmMMMmmmooooohhhh half an hour more." And then I'd go back in the kitchen and I'd do whatever, and then I'd return and I'd say, "Hunter it's time to get up." And he'd say, "Ohhhh mmmm MMmmmm give me another half hour." And I'd go back to the kitchen. So I couldn't go

anywhere. Of course I could, but I wouldn't. And when he got up, already the adrenalin had started to pump seriously in me. It was like the war has begun!

I would have gone down and gotten his newspapers, but I wouldn't talk to him. It was quiet. No. No. The TV would never be on. If somebody telephoned at that point, I would say, "Hunter is in the shower." Breakfast as I think of it, was a sacred time for him. After breakfast, he would go down in the basement, taking a beer with him. And he would pretty much stay down there. Six hours, something like that. Down there in the envelope of sensuality, the alcohol, the J.J. Cale and the smoke.

As we read Sandy's account of a typical day with Hunter, we can feel her anxiously tiptoeing around his upside down schedule and impossible demands. We can only imagine what lies behind her words like "already the adrenalin had started to pump" and "The War has begun!"

Yet in spite of all this Hunter was no monster; he was capable of great love and tenderness. Sandra goes on to say, "I was pregnant five times between 1967 and 1972. Years later, I was with Hunter and another person and I said something about "my" losing the children. And Hunter looked at me and very gently, he said, "Sandy, they were my children too." Sandra would say on a number of occasions, "He was very tender with me." "...He would just dissolve when I'd cry. He would take care of me. He would hold me and soothe me and I could count on him."

Sally Quinn, Hunter's friend, told Jean Carroll, "I always thought that Hunter was a very vulnerable sweet, gentle, kind person. He always was to me. There was something soft about him. And gentle. Underneath all that craziness...he was a gentleman. I always thought he was vulnerable, sad too. melancholy."

When Hunter was not in the grip of his craziness, he was,

in the words of Sally Quinn, "a very vulnerable, sweet, gentle, kind person." But the craziness was there, and it was a problem, a big, big problem, that finally even Sandra, great as her love was, couldn't take any longer. Sandra recalled,

> I was sitting on the floor and there was one more outburst, one more Hunter explosion, and I was really calm and I looked up at him and I said, "Hunter, I want a divorce." Just like that very calmly. Well, things kicked into gear then! He flew into a rage. I ended up calling the sheriff for help in leaving.... The deputy arrived on the porch. Hunter went to the door totally wired and turned on the charm box and said, "Oh, I'm really sorry you had to come all the way out here. This is just a little quarrel. You know how things are when the wife drinks." Well, I wanted to kill him. I hadn't had a drink in a year. Hunter went into the kitchen, and the deputy, a sweet and a very young man whispered to me. "Does he have any guns?" "Guns?" I said, "Does he have any guns? I think he has twenty two guns and every single one of them is loaded." The deputy just crumpled.
>
> I began packing. Hunter grabbed a stack of papers that I had, the only writing I had done in all those years, and threw it into the fire. I was outraged and really angry. But you know all that writing was totally pathetic. How Sandy was so little and how great Hunter was over and over again. It would be interesting to see it now, but not really interesting. He was screaming about how I would use it against him. Publish it. I'd never thought about it. He also told all our drug dealer friends that I'd turn them in.
>
> No. No. All I wanted was a little peace. So it was a fiery end. It had a fiery beginning. First time it was love. Last time it was fear.

So Sandra left him, in time they became friends, and Hunter had one girlfriend after another. Jean Carroll writes, "As Hunter gets older, his girlfriends get younger. Usually they leave him to go back to school." Margot Kidder tells about Hunter at the '84 Democratic Convention, "Hunter spent all the time at these porno shows, and he fell in love with a porno queen. Totally in love. I remember sitting one night with Hunter, and he was in tears. He was telling me how she had broken his heart. He was just devastated by this woman." Hunter was bouncing from one anima projection to another, from one devastating fantasy to the next. Years later, when they had become friends again, no longer lovers, Sandra asked Hunter, "Well, did it turn out like you thought?" And he said, "No, but," and he looked up at me with that charming smile and he said, "But it's been glamorous."

Glamorous! Hunter thinks all this intense drama is glamorous. No, no, this is a sad and tragic tale of lost love and terrible pain, which did not have to be, but Hunter clearly could never, not in this life, face what he did to the beautiful love Sandra had for him. Hunter paid a terrible price for the macho creed that says, "Real men don't need any help. They don't need to learn anything about themselves. It is all bullshit."

They have no understanding that to love is to rake up all the unfinished business from childhood, all the old rage, need, panic, insecurity and even hatred and your sexual partner becomes the focal point of it all. Sandy, speaking of the time she decided to go into therapy, said, "I did not tell Hunter because I knew he absolutely would not allow me to. Because Hunter didn't believe in therapy. He said we could handle everything ourselves. He said, It was hogwash."

Men like Hunter write off therapy and counselling because it is too great a threat to the barricade they have constructed around their old pain, their "old stuff." Hunter, when he was not in the grip of "the old stuff," was a sweet, intriguing, great guy. We all have our own brand of "old stuff," and if we are not very careful, it will bend us out of shape. The only way out is humility, determination in large doses and prayer like Hunter's prayer in <u>Fear and Loathing in Las Vegas</u>, "You better take care of me, Lord, because if you don't you're going to have me on your hands." Hunter is capable of getting a laugh from anyone, even the Creator. But Hunter was seriously in the grip of "the old stuff," and it, along with his macho pride, cost Hunter the most beautiful thing in his life: his marriage with Sandy. No college girl or porn queen or HST groupie, no matter how nubile and perky she may be, is ever going to match up to the love Sandy had for him. Hunter was bouncing from one anima projection to the next. These passions are not real; they are shimmering illusions and hopes that this will be the one who will complete and fulfill him, but it is not going to happen. No one can complete us; we have to do it for ourselves. Macho pride won't do it either. That kind of pride comes at a terrible price. Hunter paid it, and, unfortunately, so did Sandy.

Hunter and Sandy were able to be friends, because they were no longer sexually involved, and so Hunter's "stuff" is no longer stirred up by the relationship. The final question here is what drives men like Hunter? Two quotes from Jean Carroll's book give us a brief insight into that question. Bill Murray who played Hunter in the movie, "Where the Buffalo Roam," said, "The scream (Hunter will, on occasion, let lose this scream) that was my horror. The scream, that I couldn't get the scream right...It's anger and surprise and shock and pain, like a baby's scream   just a noise, a roar..." Then, Dave Burgin, an old friend of Hunter's said, "I saw Hunter at Stanford (at a speaking engagement). I was backstage with him, and he was in such a state. Agitated, absolutely paranoid. That was the day I understood that this just wasn't part of the persona. That it was serious pain. I asked him about it.

"Why do you do that at these colleges? You just drive people nuts." He said, "Cause I'm terrified."

The craziness, the guns, the sex, the drugs, the abuse, the violence, it is all a desperate attempt to keep the terror and the scream at bay. The phrase "fear and loathing" appears in two of Hunter's book titles. It recalls Kierkegaard's title, <u>Fear and Trembling: the Sickness unto Death.</u>

Hunter is another casualty of the macho male culture. He shows all the classic symptoms of a starved psyche and an anima projection: needy vulnerability, control, delusional jealousy, rages and finally the violence. Jean Carroll's book is well named, <u>Hunter: the Strange and Savage Life of Hunter S. Thompson</u>. All the first hand quoted material came from her book, which is a rare insight into a tormented soul. Highly recommended.

On October 2005, Hunter died from a self-inflicted shotgun wound to the head. One of the last things he wrote was:

Football Season is Over

No more games. No more bombs…no more fun.

Sixty seven – seventeen years past fifty…Boring…I am always bitchy.

Relax, this won't hurt.

A sad end to a great writer, a necessary talent and unique soul. His voice and vision are much needed at this particular time. He will be sadly missed by a great many of us.

CHAPTER THIRTEEN

HIS WAY, SINATRA'S WAY, MORE STRANGENESS

With some men, their anima was injured by abuse and neglect, but with others like, Frank Sinatra, who had loving, doting parents whom he loved; it was most likely caused by his own failure to care for his own soul making which deeply involves the care and cultivation of his own feminine side, his own anima making. If a man cops out on his work of soul making, something goes rotten deep inside and it permeates his entire person. It is the stunted, enraged anima churning deep down within. Frank Sinatra is an interesting study of the consequences of anima neglect and we are deeply indebted to Kitty Kelley for her brilliant book, <u>HIS WAY, the Unauthorized Biography of Frank Sinatra.</u> All of this material on Sinatra is from her valuable book.

First, we will look at Sinatra's anima projections, a sure sign of a stunted anima, then we will look at what else happens with a psyche of this sort. His relationship with Ava Gardiner has all the hallmarks of a classic projection: controlling, needy and desperate.

In her book, <u>His Way</u>, Kitty Kelley writes:

> When Ava got the part of Cynthia in "The Snows of Kilimanjaro", she was thrilled with the role, but Frank said she had to turn down it down so she could be with him in New York. "But it's the perfect part for me," she said. "The perfect part for you is being my wife," said Frank.

Ava confided her problem to the scriptwriter, Casy Robinson,

> She told me that Frank was so low; his career was so hopeless, that he needed her to go with him to New York, where he had a nightclub engagement. He insisted on it. It was quite a problem...We had to promise to shoot Ava's part in ten days. On that promise, Sinatra gave a reluctant okay. Came the ninth day of shooting. We had only one more sequence to do. Frank kept calling her on the set and making her life pretty darn miserable...I hated the little bastard because he was making my girl unhappy. Now I understand him, he was so beaten and insecure. Then came the last scene, the scene on the battlefield in Spain when Ava is dying. There was a problem: we had a great many extras, four or five hundred in all, and to satisfy the ten day agreement we'd have to shoot into the night, which would have been horribly expensive.
>
> We decided to go over the ten days and break the agreement. When King and I told Ava, all hell broke loose. She became hysterical. She called New York, and Frank was furious with her. God knows how we got through that last day.

Frank had to have this kind of control over Ava or his insecurity would drive him crazy. Frank followed Ava to the West Coast, but the volatile union erupted again days later in Palm Springs. Ava, who seemed to thrive on danger, laughed as she recalled to Kelley,

> He wanted me to go away with him someplace, but I had already arranged to be with my sister, Bappie. As usual, Frank didn't like any plan that didn't include him, so he started his usual line: "Swell, you just go off with your sister, and I'll be in Palm Springs fucking Lana Turner."
>
> ..I grabbed the car, collected Bappie, and off we drove to Palm Springs... When we got into the house, we found Lana there with Ben Cole...I hadn't been there more than ten minutes when the door bursts open and in storms Frank

looking like Al Capone and the Boston Strangler rolled into one, and starts to abuse everyone present, mostly me.

He seemed to be under the impression that we had been carving him up behind his back. He yelled at all of us and called Lana "that two bit whore," and she burst into tears and got very small and said, "I'm not going to be talked about like that," in a very little girl voice just like we were all in a Shirley Temple movie.

Frank then said to Lana, Ben, Bappie, and me, "Get the hell out of my house!" And I yelled, "Fine! But since this is also my house, too, I'm gonna take out of it everything that belongs to me." I started taking down pictures from the wall and Frank exploded. He grabbed everything I said was mine and hurled it outside onto the lawn. It was hysterical. Lana and Ben, who were both very frightened, fled from the house to look for somewhere else to stay, and when they came back for their things several hours later, we were still at it, and by that time the place was crawling with cops because the neighbors had called the police about all the noise.

Afterwards, heartsick about what had happened, Frank called Ava frequently, but she refused to answer the phone and had the number changed the next day, so he couldn't reach her. With all their plans in ruins, their trip to Ava's home in North Carolina, their trip to Africa, their baby. Frank was so distraught that according to Jimmy Van Heusen, he often vomited.

After the wrap party for "From here to Eternity", I still remember Frank sitting there telling everyone that in sixteen more hours he would be with Ava. "She's the most beautiful woman in the world. You know that, don't you," he would say. "Yes, Frank, we all know how beautiful Ava is," He would say, "She's not just one of the most beautiful women in the world; she is the most beautiful," he'd insist. He thought that he was married to the most exquisite creature on the face of the earth and he was desperately in love with her. It was kind of sad because all the rest of us knew that the marriage was held together by mere threads at that point.

That night Ava went back to the Hampshire House while Frank left to perform at the Riviera. "Stay up and wait for me, Baby," he said. But after his last show he went to Lindy's with the boys and did not show up until four A.M., which infuriated Ava, "Isn't this kind of late to be coming home?" she asked. Frank bristled. "Don't cut the corners too close on me, Baby. This is the way my life is going to be from now on."

This is the woman he maintains he loves so? These flip-flops from desperate need to angry dominating bravado are more indications of the projection. Hunter did the same thing with Sandy. The two relationships are quite parallel.

Then the newspapers reported that Ava was seen dining quietly with Peter Lawford (an old friend of both Ava and Frank's) at Frascati's in Los Angeles...Frank flew into a rage and called Lawford, threatening him. "Oh, God, he was furious with me for going out with Ava," said Peter Lawford many years later. He screamed, "Do you want your legs broken, you fucking asshole? Well, you're going to get them broken if I ever hear you're out with Ava again. So help me, I'll kill you. Do you hear me?" Then he slammed the phone down. I was panicked. I mean I was really scared. Frank's a violent guy and he's good friends with too many guys who'd rather kill you than say hello. I didn't want to die, so I called Jimmy Van Heusen and said, "Please tell him nothing happened. Please." Jimmy said not to worry. That Frank would get over it. He knew we'd been friends since 1945. Well, Frank got over it all right, but it took him six years!"

This is not normal behavior. Of course, nearly everyone gets angry at some time or another, but treating an old friend like this, not talking to Lawford for six years! Threatening him with such violence that he was afraid for his life! Even in our society, with its tolerance for violence, this is not normal behavior. Likewise, the fear Lana Turner and Ben Cole felt during the incident at Palm Springs testify to the depth of these nearly insane furies of Sinatra's. These turbulent emotions swirling about Ava, lashing out at anyone or anything are more evidence of Frank's projection and the violence associated with it.

Out of his mind with grief over Ava, Frank flew to New York enroute to a nightclub engagement at the Chase Hotel in St. Louis. He wandered around Manhattan like one of the dammed, filled with remorse and self-pity, unable to focus on anything but this terrible personal loss...

On November 18, 1953, Jimmy Van Heusen, who had an apartment on Fifty Seventh Street, found Frank on the floor of the elevator with his wrists slashed. Van Heusen immediately called a doctor and rushed Frank to Mt. Siani Hospital, but not before paying the man at the front desk of his building fifty dollars to keep quiet about the incident.

The nights were the hardest for Frank. An old friend of Frank's told Kelley,

> One time he called us over to play cards...By the time we got there the game started, he didn't even want to play anymore. He went into the den, opened a bottle and started drinking alone. Okay. So we keep the game going awhile, and then Sammy Cahn gets up and he goes in to try to get Frank to join us. So what does he see?
>
> There's Frank drinking a toast to a picture of Ava with a tear running down his face. So Sammy comes back and we start playing again. All of a sudden we hear a crash. We all get up and run into the den, and there's Frank. He had taken the picture of Ava, frame and all, and smashed it. Then he had picked up the picture, ripped it into little pieces, and thrown it on the floor. So we tell him, "Come on, Frank, you've got forget about all that. Come on any play some cards with us." He says, "I'm through with her. I never want to see her again.

I'm all right. I've just been drinking too much."

So we go back to the game and a little while later Sammy goes back to Frank, and there he is on his hands and knees picking up the torn pieces of the picture and trying to put it back together again. Well, he gets all the pieces together except the one for the nose. He becomes frantic looking for it, and we all get down on our hands and knees and try to help him.

All of a sudden, the doorbell rings. It's the delivery boy with more liquor. So Frank goes to the back door to let him in, but when he opens it, the missing piece flutters out. Well, Frank is so happy, he takes off his gold wristwatch and gives it to the delivery boy.

This crushing, enduring despair, these wild swings of mood are the stuff of anima projection. It is not about lost love. Their relationship was more a bitter fight than of love. The comedian, Shecky Greene, said something revealing to Kitty Kelley, "He always told me one of the things that fascinated him about Ava was that there was no conquest. He couldn't conquer her. That is where the respect comes. He never got her. He couldn't control or dominate her. He'd get drinking and tell me how she always called him a goddamned hoodlum and a gangster. He'd never take that from anyone else but Ava. She was always a challenge to him..."

Greene calls it respect; he didn't know what else to call it. Because Sinatra never had a real relationship with Ava, the projection never had a chance to break down. Day to day living with someone relating to the real person behind the projection breaks it down and the actual person starts to emerge. Then and only then does the real relationship begin or not depending on the one's choice to do so.

Sometimes the projection is quick then breaks down just as quickly. A lady friend of Jimmy Van Heusen's told Kitty

Kelley about Frank's "before and after treatment."

> ...It was really something to see. Frank would bring someone to the desert for the weekend... Before bed he would so charming. The girl was "Mademoiselle this," "Darling that,' and "My sweet baby.' He was a cavalier, a perfect gentleman. You never saw anything like this man in your life. He'd jump across the room to light a cigarette. He'd fill her glass with champagne every time she took a sip. With a hand on her neck he'd say, "You're beautiful tonight or he'd whisper loud enough for all of us to hear, "No one prettier has ever been to my house. You look radiant, gorgeous."
>
> Then the next day we'd go over for his interminal pool party, where everyone drank for hours... It was the next day that we'd always find the other Frank, the one who wouldn't speak to the girl, who had been the most beautiful woman in the world the night before. Sometimes he wouldn't go near her, nor would he tolerate any affectionate overtures from her. Humped and dumped. The minute the conquest was achieved, kaput. The girl could pack her bags. I saw so many of them leave his house in tears.

Frank was not about love, sex or conquest. He was hoping this new girl would fill the void left in him by Ava, that she would be his new anima. When she failed to achieve that for him, he was angry and she was dumped. Judith Campbell said, "He was Dr. Jekyll and Mr. Hyde, and sometimes you wouldn't know which one you were going to get. Frank's Mr. Hyde was a charmer, but his Dr. Jekyll was frightening, truly frightening."

Sinatra and Hunter Thompson both exhibit this same pattern. Wonderful, charming, devoted attention and affection, then it mysteriously goes wrong. The initial phase is the courtship of the anima, which they have projected onto the woman. The second phase is the anima lashing back for she will accept no substitutes and it gets ugly. The void in these men is still there and it ravages them.

Sinatra's history with women, particularly with Ava, indicates a strong anima projection operating within his psyche, but projection is not the only consequence of a stunted anima development. Sinatra's rages were not ordinary temper; they come from somewhere deeper than that.

Brad Dexter, a film producer who courageously saved Sinatra from drowning and who for a while was a favorite friend of Frank's, had this to say about him,

> After awhile I could see it coming. I could tell in Frank's eyes when that terrible mood change was about to happen. There is some emotional conflict deep inside him that is triggered off by God knows what, and when it comes rushing to the surface, he explodes and hurts someone either physically or psychologically. Frank is a true manic-depressive and careens from great waves of elation to bouts of morose despair. Like the time he urinated on Lee Mortimer's grave. Afterwards he screamed, "I'll bury the bastards, I'll bury them all."

Peter Lawford recalled Sinatra's treatment of his old friend Sammie Davis Jr.,

> ....It could have been a lot worse given Frank's temper. You have no idea of that temper. He can get so mad that he is driven to real violence... I know. I've seen it. One time at a party in Palm Springs, he got so mad at some poor girl that he slammed her through a plate glass window. There was shattered glass and blood all over the place and the girl's arm was nearly severed from her body. Jimmy Van Heusen rushed her to the hospital. Frank paid her off and the whole thing was hushed up, of course, but I remember Judy Garland and I looking at each other and shivering with fright at the time. I did everything I could to avoid setting off that temper...

"Temper"- no, this is beyond temper; this is violence, from a disturbed personality.

Jacqueline Park, speaking of Frank, said,

> There were a lot of women who fell in love with Frank, but He'd reject them and throw them over. There's a monster in him who wants to screw the world before it screws him, hurt people before they hurt him. Then he feels guilty about being so ugly and that guilt makes him a Mr. Nice Guy and so he does favors for some of the girls he's used or rejected. When Joi Lansing, who was a regular bed mate of Frank's for years, was dying of leukemia, he paid for of all her hospital bills.

Brad Dexter and Peter Lawford have seen Sinatra being taken over by some malevolent spirit. It is the anima down there in the basement of Frank's psyche where she has been locked down and like a hungry dog getting meaner and meaner. She takes her vengeance with these obsessive rages, depressions, and jealousies. There is a parallel here between the behavior of Sinatra and Hunter Thompson; they both have wild swings of mood toward women; they both suffered the ravages of the anima.

Jung's on this from <u>The Collected Works,</u>

> Everything the anima touches becomes ...unconditional, dangerous, taboo, magical...She...would break down our moral inhibitions and unleash forces that had better been left undisturbed (CW 9, i, 59). ....With this anima., then we plunge straight into the ancient world, (CW 12, 112) ...into the ancient world of myth and mysterious forces, into the mind of our unknown ancestors (CW 9, i, 518). She drives us crazy at the same time she drives us to higher levels of meaningful and felt wisdom.

Jung would have the anima represented by "the four female figures of the Gnostic underworld, Eve, Helen of Troy, Mary, and Sophia (Goddess of Wisdom). Jung's notion of the anima is no easy matter. Let it suffice that the anima is a serious force in the psyche of any man, a force to be reckoned. Woe betide any man who has not established a good relationship with his own feminine because the anima and the animus are so intertwined that if the anima is stunted she will contaminate his masculine as well. His entire psyche will be distorted.

Kitty Kelley goes on to say, "In his manic phase Frank seemed like the greatest Italian host since Lorenzo de Medici. He spent money lavishly, wining and dining his friends with unstinting generosity, flying them around the world in his private plane, swamping them with expensive gifts. He tipped waitresses and hatcheck girls with handfuls of hundred dollar bills."

There is a desperation in these wild swings of mood. This is Sinatra's anima lashing back at him, but the essential point, is that there is nothing romantic about these wild swings of mood. They are indications of deep trouble in a man you want nothing to do with. This is not romantic even though the manic highs of a man like this can be very seductive. Frank was able to win the love of a number of wonderful, attractive, intelligent women: Lauren Bacall, Elizebeth Taylor, Judy Garland, Natlie Wood and others. The list goes on and on. He was engaging and winning, but what did it mean? What was behind it? He was not relating to the actual person in these relationships; he was relating to the image he had projected on them. That is what they do: Sinatra, Hunter and the rest of them. Ava was Sinatra's true anima image. The others were merely desperate substitutes and once he possessed them, he knew they were not The One.

We are deeply indebted to Kitty Kelley for these excerpts from her book, His Way. Her book is well worth reading in its entirety. Sinatra fought the publication with all the resources at his command: his wealth, his lawyers, his influence, his fame, but he could not do it. The Reporters Committee for Freedom of the Press, the Society of Professional Journalists, the Newspaper Guild, PEN, the American Society of Journalists and Authors, the National Writers Union, the Council of Writers Organization all supported Kelley. It took courage to go up against Sinatra. Many of her sources were too frightened of Sinatra to go on record, but, for once, his way did not prevail. These excerpts just give a sample of the value and excellence of the entire book. It is a brilliant study of a male psyche out of balance and how that man could be so winning, but a disaster for any woman involved with him.

Jung saw the source of the craziness we see in Sinatra, O.J. Simpson, Hunter Thompson, Constable Hotte and the rest. It is far more complex than simple sexual frustration. These men had a number of attractive women available to them. Jung understands the demonic power of the denied anima which has racked these men and which will rack any man who denies his feminine. These men expect a woman to fill their emptiness. It does not work like that. No woman can. They have not done their soul work and only they can do it. There are no substitutes, no short cuts or an outraged anima will drive the man to project his idealized anima onto some woman. He will then be driven to possess her, but he never will. His whole self will be disturbed and volatile. Neither he nor his partner will have any peace. The furies will turn on him and he will turn on the woman, and his men friends as well.

The denied anima can do more than create these obsessions and distorted reality around a woman. Jung wrote, "The anima is the energy of the heavy and the turbid...Its effects are sensuous desires and impulses to anger." We have seen these same "sensuous desires and impulses to anger" at work in Frank Sinatra and Hunter Thompson and the rest of these men. A warning comes through Jung's careful academic language: the anima is not to be taken lightly. It is a force to be reckoned.

Jung had some withering observations on Western civilization and thought:

> Christian civilization has proved hollow to a terrifying degree: it is all veneer, but the inner man has remained untouched and therefore unchanged...Inside reign the archaic gods, supreme as of old..."(CW 12, 12). Spiritually the Western world is in a precarious situation, and the danger is greater the more we blind ourselves.... Western man lives in a thick cloud of incense which he burns to himself so that his own countenance may be veiled from him in the smoke.... that megalomania of ours which leads us to suppose... that Christianity is the only truth and the white Christ is the only redeemer. No wonder that unearthing the psyche is like undertaking a full scale drainage operation." (CW 10, 183 86)

I think there is a distinction to be made between the teachings and life of Jesus and the culture and the civilization, which has accumulated down through history in his name. They are quite different entities. Jung saw the staggering difficulty of overhauling the psyche and culture of Western Man, a civilization largely formed by the patriarchal mind.

These men we have studied: Sinatra, Thompson, O.J. Simpson and the rest do not appear to be happy men. Suppressing the feminine in a man's life diminishes his capacity for love, happiness and the fullness of life.

President Reagan gave the Presidential Medal of Freedom to Sinatra and Stevens Institute of Technology awarded him with an honorary Doctorate, in spite of the protest of over a hundred graduating seniors. President Reagan, as he placed the beribboned medal around Frank's neck, intoned these words: "His love of country, his generosity for those less fortunate, his distinctive art, and his winning and compassionate persona make him one of our most remarkable and distinguished Americans and one who truly did it his way."

Garry Trudeau brilliantly satirized this farce in his cartoon strip, "Doonesbury." Kitty Kelley included them in her book. Not to be missed. The institutions and the culture, which have honored Sinatra, the Republican Party and the University, are citadels of male culture. Only a culture, which is deeply flawed, could have honored a man so deeply flawed himself. The lapse of consciousness exhibited in these two awards staggers the mind as does the aura given to Sinatra's signature song, "My Way, I Did it My Way", like it was some kind of theme of the noble individualist. A way to be emulated by men everywhere. But then lack of consciousness and its ugly consequences are exactly what we have been talking about.

CHAPTER FOURTEEN

The Dream Gone Wrong

Norman Mailer's novel, <u>An American Dream</u>, is the story of a love gone seriously wrong. Steve Rojack is on his way over to Debora Kelley's apartment. His gut is churning as he mulls over their relationship. He doesn't know it yet, but once there he will strangle her and then throw her dead body out of the window to the street ten floors below. He is deep in the trance and hell of an anima projection and all the devastation that goes with it is upon him.

Let me not be all dead," I cried to myself... I was sick ... I was sick in a way I had never been sick before. Deep in a fever ... one's soul could always speak to one. "Look what this illness is doing to us, you coward."... I could feel what was good in me going away... my courage, my wit, ambition and hope... I flew down the stairs pursued by panic, because I had lost my sense of being alive and here on earth, it was more as if I had died and did not altogether know it... A familiar misery was upon me. I was separate from Debora as much as a week or two at a time, but there would come a moment, there would always come a moment...when it was impossible not to call her. At moments like that I would feel as if I had committed hari kari and was walking about with my chest separated from my groin.... it was the remains of my love for her, love draining from the wound, leaving behind its sense of desolation as if all the love I possessed were being lost...

So I hated her, yes indeed I did, but my hatred was a cage... I did not know if I had the force to find my way free. Marriage to her was the armature of my ego, remove the armature and I might topple like clay... when she loved me ... her strength seemed to pass to mine and I was live with wit, I had vitality, I could depend on stamina, I possessed my style.... the gift was only up for loan. The instant she stopped loving me... why then my psyche was whisked off stage and stuffed in a pit. A devil's contract, and during all of this last year, not living with her and yet never separated...I would, nevertheless, be dropped suddenly into an hour where all of my substance fell out of me and I had to see her. I had a physical need to see her as direct as an addict's panic waiting for his drug.

Arriving there it goes badly. She says to him, "Because you know I don't love you any more at all." "She said it so quietly, with such a nice finality. ...I had opened a void. I was now without a center. Can you understand? I did not belong to myself any longer. Debora had occupied my center... Yes, the center was gone..."

They say terrible things to each other as they dance a dance of a thousand cuts, and then Rojack can't take any more.

I struck her open handed across the face. I some last calm intention of my mind had meant to make it no more than a slap, but my body was speaking faster than my brain, and the blow caught her on the side of the ear and knocked her half out of bed....

...That blew it out. I struck her a blow on the back of the neck, a dead cold chop which dropped her to a knee, and then hooked an arm about her head and put a pressure on her throat.... For ten or twenty seconds she strained in balance, and then her strength began to pass, it passed over to me, and I felt my arm tightening about her neck. My eyes were closed. .... My mind then cried out, Hold back! You're going too far, hold back!"...I was trying to stop, but pulse packed behind pulse...some black biled lust, some desire to go ahead...came bursting with rage out of me and my mind exploded in a fireworks of rockets, stars, and hurtling embers, the arm about her neck leaped against the whisper I could still feel murmuring in her throat, and, crack, I choked her harder...and, crack, I gave her payment never halt now.... I was floating. I was as far into myself as I had ever been.... I opened my eyes. I was weary with a most honorable fatigue, and my flesh seemed new... But there was Debora, dead beside me on the flowered carpet of the floor... She was dead, indeed she was dead.

I have been there. I remember what it was like when I was projecting the goddess onto Eileen, then Marnie, then Nancy, Dianne and Susan. When it was good, I was filled with joy, vitality and confidence. My life, my very being, was expanded and filled with joy and promise. It was as if every cell in my body, every synapse, was wonderfully alive and vibrating with love and life. It was the wildest narcotic in the world; it was Love Potion Number Nine. I had made these women into goddesses and given them the power to bestow divine bliss unto me, and to transport me out of ordinary life and up into the realm of the gods. I gave them my power. But when the relationship died, it all went away and a part of me died with it. All the wonder and life I had felt when I was with her was gone. It was as though a plug deep down in my pelvic basin had been pulled and it all drained out.

Mailer got it right in <u>Dream</u>, "Marriage to her was the armature of my ego, remove the armature and I might topple like clay." That is how it was. I felt devastated and empty with nothing to give. Nothing vital or of interest was in me. There was nothing to give to her. I couldn't bear being with her feeling that empty, being that empty, even though I desperately wanted to see her and to be with her. I could think of nothing else.: What was she doing? What was she thinking? Should I call? What would I say? And all the while, my life was totally empty. I had given away the power of my life. After Eileen had gone, it was February; I wrote in my journal, "The sun is gone from my winter sky." I was a strung out love junkie. The drop from cloud nine was long and hard. My mind had been taken over by some kind of mysterious and mythic power. Then with Christine and Dianne I felt all that along with a deep and terrible rage. It was totally beyond any disappointment, frustration or discouragement. It was devastation. It was nothing about love; it was some kind of mythic trance. It was the first time I had wanted to do anyone any serious harm. If I had not had the psychological and spiritual resources, which were there for me, I could have ended up in the newspapers. It could have been very bad.

The anima projection denies us love and throws us into its dark storm. With Rojack, Mailer has brilliantly portrayed the ravages and compulsion of the Anima projection. When it was good, it was very good: "When she loved me...her strength seemed to pass to mine and I was alive with wit...." But when it was over, "I was sick in a way I had never been sick before," "...the armature of my ego, remove the armature and I might topple like clay," and he was filled with "some black biled lust," and he was, "as far into myself as I had ever been..." This is the stuff of nightmares, the nightmare of the anima projection, and Mailer got it right. Its all there: the emptiness, the dependency on the woman for feeling alive and the blind, dangerous rage when it is over and gone.

CHAPTER FIFTEEN

Parsifal, Everyman and the Holy Grail

John A. Sanford's introduction to Robert Johnson's <u>He: Understanding Male Psychology</u> is a profound and clarifying statement.

> A central idea in Jung's psychology is his concept of individuation. Individuation is the lifelong process in which a person becomes whole and complete... It entails the gradual expansion of his or her consciousness and the increasing capacity of the conscious personality to reflect the total self. The Ego may be understood as the center of the consciousness, the "I" within us that part of ourselves with which we are consciously identified. The self is the name given to the total personality, the potential person who is within us from the beginning and seeks in our lifetime to be recognized and expressed through the ego.
>
> The individuation process, which is the realization of the potential self, involves the individual in psychological and spiritual problems of great complexity. One difficult problem is always the matter of becoming reconciled with the shadow-the dark, unwanted dangerous side of our selves that conflicts with our conscious attitudes and ideals, but with which everyone must somehow come to terms if she or he is to become whole.

The rejection of the shadow personality results in a division within the personality and the establishment of a state of hostility (and hence rejection-PMH) between the conscious and the unconscious. Acceptance and integration of these two components of the psyche is never easy but even more difficult is a man's inclusion of his unconscious feminine element. The inner woman in a man Jung calls the anima. Because of this difficulty, the inner woman in man is frequently rejected and even despised. Her very existence is denied.

We have seen evidence of that denial in the military and other bastions of the macho world. Johnson believes that myth serves the same function to the collective unconscious of mankind as the dream serves to the individual. Our dreams come forth from our unconscious as it works to express an urgent psychological truth to us. Johnson sees the myth of Parsifal's search for the Holy Grail as an urgent message from the collective male unconscious of the necessity that we males include and embrace our feminine self, and this chapter is indebted to Dr. Johnson's invaluable book, which helped me greatly in my own quest.

The Holy Grail legend is about the mystery and sacred quest for wholeness. Parsifal is every man on the long and arduous path to fulfill his manhood. Parsifal's struggles and trials symbolically represent the long path every man must travel. The Holy Grail and the tradition of Courtly Love, which came in at about the same time, are both about the quest for unity with the inner feminine.

First, Parsifal must leave his mother, which is a major event in any man's psychic life. He goes to King Arthur's court and tells the Knights of the Round Table he wants to be a knight. They see a country bumpkin standing there in his mother's homespun garment and they laugh. Red Knight has been ravaging the countryside and insulting Arthur and Queen Guenevere. No knight of the Round Table has been able to stand up to him. As a mocking joke, they tell Parsifal, "If you kill the Red Knight, we will make you a knight."

Then he says to King Arthur, "If I kill the Red Knight, I want his horse and armor." Arthur laughs and says, "You have my permission if you can get it." Parsifal departs and soon encounters the Red Knight. He challenges him and the two square off. Parsifal is knocked to the ground and the Red Knight is about to kill him as Parsifal draws his knife and throws it. The knife pierces through the eye of the Red Knight killing him. This is an important symbolic event. The Red Knight symbolizes the shadow masculine energy, energy, which cannot be repressed or lost, or he will be emasculated. It must be conquered and then utilized because a man needs the energy of the masculine shadow to make his way to mature full manhood.

So now, Parsifal owns the Red Knight's armor and warhorse but the straps and fittings of the armor are unfamiliar and confusing to him, but a page who came out to see the combat helps and teaches him how to don the armor. He also recommends that he take off his mother's homespun garment that is unbefitting a knight. Parsifal refuses. His mother's homespun garment represents the mother complex. This is the temptation in a man to retain the dependent relationship he had with his mother with her taking care of him. He mounts the horse, but no one has taught him how to stop. He rides all day until they both stop from exhaustion. Both the horse and the armor symbolize his shadow masculine energy, which he has not yet integrated with his self.

On his travels, he comes upon the hermit, Gournamond, who becomes like a godfather, teaching him the ways of knighthood. He must never seduce or be seduced by a fair maiden. He must seek the Grail Castle with all his might and when he gets there, he is to ask a certain question, "Whom does the Grail serve?" After a year, Gournamond sends him on his way.

He comes upon Blanche Fleur, which means white flower. She is in distress for her castle is under siege. He comes to her rescue doing battle with the knights besieging her kingdom, one at a time, then sparing their lives with their promise to serve King Arthur, which adds to the power and fellowship of the Round Table. Johnson wrote:

> This is a poetic way of describing the process Dr. Jung speaks of as 'relocating the center of gravity of the personality,' a careful and highly conscious process of drawing from the untamed pool of masculine energy and adding to the conscious center of the personality, which is here represented by King Arthur and the Round Table.

This "relocating the center of the personality," this forming, shaping and directing the raw, untamed masculine energy is a profound event in the process of the male psyche. It is a further refining of the masculine shadow energy.

After raising the siege of her castle, Parsifal spends one night with Blanch Fleur. He heeds Gournamond's instructions and they sleep head-to-head, shoulder-to-shoulder, hip-to-hip, knee-to-knee, toe-to-toe. But their embrace is chaste and worthy of his vow. Blanche is not to be considered a flesh and blood woman. She is the inner feminine. She is the fountain of life in the heart of man. She is the very core of inspiration. She is the Anima and he cannot stay with her. Above all, he must not attempt to seduce her for to do so is to confuse two of the six aspects of the feminine within a man: the inner feminine with one's wife or mate. Men who do this betray their wives with affairs with their students, secretaries or younger women. Almost always, it is disastrous.

Parsifal must go on. He rides all day. At nightfall, he asks if there is anywhere he can stay. He is told there is no habitation within thirty miles. A little while later, he comes to a lake. There is a man in a boat fishing. Parsifal asks him if there is anywhere to stay the night. The fisherman, who is the Fisher King, invites him to stay with him. "Just go down the road a little way, turn left, cross the drawbridge. He follows the directions and as he crosses the drawbridge, it snaps shut just ticking the rear hooves of his horse. "It is dangerous to enter the grail castle for that is the Fisher King's home, and many a youth is unhorsed as he makes the transition from our ordinary world into the imaginary, symbolic world of the Grail Castle."

Parsifal finds himself in the keep of a great castle where four youths take his horse, bathe him, give him fresh clothing, and lead him to the master of the castle, the Fisher King. The King apologizes for being unable to rise from his litter and greet Parsifal properly due to his wound. The whole court of the castle, four hundred knights and ladies is there to greet Parsifal, and wonderful ceremony takes place.

In a setting of such grandeur, one knows that Parsifal has blundered into the inner world, the place of the spirit, the place of transformation. Especially when the number four is accentuated four hundred knights and ladies, four youths, the great fireplace with four faces showing the cardinal directions.

The Fisher King lies groaning in agony on his litter, one fair maiden carries in the lance that pierced the side of Christ, another fair maiden brings in the paten from which the last supper was served, and finally a third maiden brings in the Holy Grail itself. (Here is the correct place for the interior woman in a man's psychology. She, who is the mediator for him to the numinous values of the inner world.)

They are all waiting to see if he is the innocent fool of the legend, which foretold he would come to the Grail Castle, and ask the sacred question, which would heal the Fisher King. Unless the question is asked, the great bounty of the Grail cannot come forth and the Fisher King cannot be healed. That bounty is nothing less than the cornucopia of life itself. It is the fullness of life on every level, material and spiritual.

When he was leaving home, Parsifal's mother told him not to ask too many questions. In general, good advice to a young man, but not here as Parsifal stands mute before all the splendour and expectation of the Grail castle. It is a time for him to assert his manhood, but he chooses his mother's council over Gournamond's. He fails to ask the question.

The Fisher King, groaning and writhing in agony is taken to his chamber. All the knights and ladies disperse and Parsifal is escorted to his room by four young men.

The next morning Parsifal awakes to find himself alone. He saddles his horse and rides out over the drawbridge, which snaps shut behind him, ticking the hooves of his horse behind him. It is another profound transition and Parsifal is back in the ordinary world. There is no castle to be seen. Parsifal has failed the test and he has been removed from the mystical and glorious world of the Grail castle because he still wears under his armor the one-piece homespun garment, which his mother gave him. He has not matured out of his mother complex.

It causes him to reject his mature masculinity. "It is pure poison in a man's psychology." I have a friend, Norman, when he walks in the room with his boyish charm, big smile and entertaining patter, you'd think that the circus has come to town. He sweeps women away with all this, moves in with them, then blows up the relationship with the dependency he dumps on them. He is a charming infant, but in a grown man, you cannot stand it. He gets himself fired from one job after another with a mix of childish rebellion and know-it-all incompetence. Johnson is right on calling it "pure poison." It is self-sabotage of our male maturity, and there is a lot of it around. See Johnson's Lying With The Heavenly Maiden for a discussion of the several aspects of the feminine in a man and the complications, which can occur when they are confused one with the other. Very valuable.

The legend maintains that most young men have a brief taste of the full possibilities of life, but lack the maturity and wisdom to sustain it, so like Parsifal they find themselves outside the Grail castle trying to find their way back. Like Parsifal, for decades we wander looking for the Grail. There are many false grails. For Andrew Fastow, Jeff Skilling and the rest of those, it was wealth and power. For other men it is to have a woman serve as their flesh and blood Blanch Fleur. They make her into their grail. We seek our inner feminine with an Anima Projection. It is one of the confusions of the six feminine elements in a man's psychic life, a confusion which is disastrous.

Parsifal has left the Grail Castle and now must earn the right to return to it. For twenty years, he wanders through a long series of knight's ventures that gradually strengthen him for a second entrance to the Grail Castle, but it has been very hard. Doubt and despair weigh heavily upon him. During this time, Parsifal has removed the homespun garment woven by his mother. Parsifal then comes upon a band of ragged pilgrims who are wandering on the road. They say to him, "What are doing riding in full armor on this, the day of the death of our Lord? Don't you know it is Good Friday? Come with us to the forest hermit to say your confession and be shriven in preparation for Easter Sunday." They awaken something deep in Parsifal and he goes with them to meet the Hermit in the Forest.

The Hermit instantly sees Parsifal with clairvoyant sight and berates him for all his faults and failures the worst of which was at the Grail Castle. That done, he grows gentle with Parsifal, points down the road, "Go a short way, turn left, cross the drawbridge." The Grail Castle is always close at hand, just down the road to those humble and of good heart.

Here the great French poem by Cretien stops quite mysteriously. Perhaps now the story is no longer Parsifal's but ours. Are we going to enter the Grail Castle to ask this strange and mysterious question?

Sometimes to ask the question is to arrive at the answer at the same time. The Grail will not serve modern man's self-centered notion of happiness. It will not serve Dennis Kozlowski of Tyco International LTD in his quest for $6,000 shower curtains and $16,000 umbrella stands. It will not serve the I-me notion of happiness of these men. George Bernard Shaw wrote, "The direct pursuit of happiness is folly." But when our Grail serves the higher self, the self of which Jung speaks, then we:

> ...make our own soul through all our earthly days, and at the same time collaborate in another work, in another opus, which infinitely transcends... our individual achievement: the completing of the world... Beneath our efforts to put spiritual form into our lives, the world slowly accumulates...that which will make of it... the new earth.

>   de Chardin

The significance of the wounded Fisher King is not easy. If the Fisher King is God, how is God wounded, suffering, and needing our commitment to heal? The Lost Will books received by Ceanne DeRohan portray the Father wrestling with his own self-discovery and evolution, particularly with his own inner feminine, which took the Father a long time to understand. Now we are all involved, together with God, in some kind of cosmic evolution. The whole of creation proceeds out of this evolution. I find it pretty scary stuff, and overwhelming, the notion that we are all working it out together. It is not easy to understand these things. From some where way back I dimly recall a line of poetry, maybe Keats, "The world groans in travail for completion," and somehow God together with all of us are involved in this agony of birth and creation. I can't escape the feeling that the stakes in our own evolution are higher than we know. I recall Jung on the Self:

> The self is the name given to the total personality, the potential person who is within us from the beginning and seeks in our lifetime to be recognized and expressed through the ego.

This self is sacred. It is the part of us that is involved in the process described earlier by de Chardin. It is the part of us that is in the image of the Father.

In our commitment to the self and the larger work of the self, I believe, is the answer to the riddle and mystery of the Grail question. Goethe ends <u>Faust</u> with, "The Eternal Feminine draws us onward." The cultivation of the self is our divinely appointed life's work. It is the Grail quest.